Camp GLOW
(Girls Leading Our World)
Handbook
for
Volunteers

Peace Corps

October 2001

Information Collection and Exchange
Publication Number M0056

ACKNOWLEDGMENTS

The *Camp GLOW Handbook for Volunteers* was compiled and adapted from materials developed by Peace Corps Volunteers and staff including: Camp GLOW manuals from Poland and Romania; Project Status Reports from Bulgaria, Kazakhstan, Latvia, Madagascar, Mali, South Africa, Slovakia, and Uzbekistan; proposals and reports from Armenia, the Kyrgyz Republic, Morocco, and the Philippines; and Emails, especially from Sarah Goodkind for the history section; Susan Grove for the cultural understanding, GLOW Clubs, and junior counselors sections; and Chris Kanstrup for the financial resources section. The Peace Corps gratefully acknowledges the authors of those materials.

This publication was developed by the following team: Amy Nahley for research and writing; Kitty Andang, Judee Blohm, Justine Ickes, Jonathon Landeck, and Amy Stevens for rewrites and editing; in collaboration with the Women in Development/Gender and Development Specialist, Lyn Messner, in the Center for Field Assistance and Applied Research, Peace Corps/Washington.

TABLE OF CONTENTS

How to Use this Handbook 1

Background 1

CHAPTER 1: PLANNING
Camp GLOW Timeline 5
Leadership within the Organizing Committee 9
Needs Assessment 10
Establishing Goals 11
Identifying Partners 13
Creating a Budget 13
Identifying a Campsite 15

CHAPTER 2: LOGISTICS
Tips for Smooth Logistics 16
Supplies 17
Selecting Campers, Junior Counselors, Counselors 18
Potential Resources 20
    People 20
    Ideas for Fundraising 22
Sources of Information 24
    Internet 24
    Publications 25
    ICE Resources 25

CHAPTER 3: ACTIVITIES FOR IMPLEMENTATION
Developing a Schedule 29
    Tips for Scheduling 29
Activities 31
    Management Activities 31
    Opening Activities 33
    Activities for Special Purposes 33
    Closing Activities 51

CHAPTER 4: APPLICATIONS OF CAMP GLOW
Environment 53
Health 54
Teaching English as a Foreign Language.. 54
Involving Boys and Men in Camp GLOW 55
Cultural Understanding 56
Democracy Building 57

CHAPTER 5: AT THE END OF CAMP
Celebration 59
Evaluation 59
Reporting 60

CHAPTER 6: TAKING THE EXPERIENCE HOME
On-going Activities with Campers 62
    GLOW Clubs 62
    Follow-up with Teachers, Parents, Community 65
    Junior Counselors 66
    Email Discussion Group 66
Wrap Up/Conclusion 66

APPENDICES
Appendix A: Budget A-1
Appendix B: Schedules of Activities A-2
Appendix C: Packing List for Campers A-5
Appendix D: Flyer A-6
Appendix E: Camp GLOW Application, Evaluation Form, and Acceptance, Wait-list and Non-acceptance Letters A-7
Appendix F: Camp GLOW Permission Slip and Medical Information A-12
Appendix G: Letters to English Teachers Requesting Nominations of Campers A-13
Appendix H: Peace Corps Partnership Reporting Guidelines and Sample Proposal A-15
Appendix I: Certificates A-22
Appendix J: Evaluation Form A-24
Appendix K: Compilation of Camp GLOW Evaluations A-25
Appendix L: Thank You Notes from Volunteers and Campers A-27
Appendix M: How to Form a GLOW Club in your School A-28

CAMP GLOW HANDBOOK FOR VOLUNTEERS

HOW TO USE THIS HANDBOOK

Previous and current Volunteers' experiences are the basis of this **Handbook**. You will find examples from different posts, suggestions of activities and tips for organizing your own camp. The **Handbook** is organized in chronological order in terms of planning a Camp GLOW (Girls Leading Our World), although many activities take place simultaneously. The appendices may serve as a template for the paperwork surrounding your camp. The appendices include materials such as camp applications, invitations, and certificates. The book is yours to print, copy, and tailor the contents to meet your needs.

BACKGROUND

History of Camp GLOW

Camp GLOW (Girls Leading Our World) began in Romania in 1995. Three Volunteers and four Romanian teachers took 80 young women to a mountain campsite for a weeklong leadership camp. The purpose of this camp was to encourage young women to become active citizens by building their self-esteem and confidence, increasing their self-awareness, and developing their skills in goal setting, assertiveness, and career and life planning.

In Romania, the idea for Camp GLOW rose out of community needs and the trends observed by the original organizers. These needs and trends included:

- Women working outside the home seemed not to affect traditional gender roles inside the home. In other words, most women did all or most of the cleaning, laundry, cooking, and childcare. Thus, women were solely responsible for two jobs.

- Students seemed to accept these traditional roles.

- There was a lack of positive female role models in politics or in other public positions of power.

- Students seemed to lack leadership skills and initiative to make active decisions that would positively impact their lives and their country's future.

The first Camp GLOW in Romania was a resounding success. One Romanian Volunteer said, "The energy and intellect of the campers is inspirational. When I think of the campers, the future of Romania looks bright. Camp GLOW was one of the highlights of my Peace Corps service."

Since that first camp in Romania, Peace Corps has actively supported Camp GLOW in other Peace Corps countries. In the year 2000, approximately 21 camps took place around the world.[1] In each country Peace Corps Volunteers and host-country nationals have adapted Camp GLOW to reflect the realities of the young women in their local communities. While the content and styles of Camp GLOW vary, certain principles and themes exist through all of the camps. These principles and themes include developing leadership skills, improving self-esteem, increasing knowledge of women's health issues, respecting and caring for the environment, and promoting the belief that every young woman can make a difference in her community.

Today, Camp GLOW continues to be seen as an ideal way to offer adolescent girls self-development opportunities in a fun and friendly atmosphere. In the *Camp GLOW Grant Proposal* for Armenia for example, the organizers state "future female leaders are currently held back by not only a lack of information concerning career options, but also a culturally induced lack of support for strong, enterprising women. Due to a current lack of exploration in the fields of leadership skills, career options, and psychological development, we feel a women's leadership camp would be beneficial to the young leaders of Armenia."

Why Camp GLOW?

Participating in Camp GLOW is often a life changing experience for both the adult organizers and the teen-age campers. It also develops community leaders and builds cross-cultural bridges. As one camper said in her evaluation of the camp, "I've learned to be more open, to establish my goals, to work as a team, and to trust myself."

Camp GLOW falls within the Congressional mandate that "the Peace Corps shall be administered so as to give particular attention to those programs, projects and activities which tend to integrate women into the national economies of developing countries, thus improving their status and assisting in the total development effort."[2] Camp GLOW meets this mandate by providing a forum for girls to share, grow, and develop skills in a variety of areas that allow them to take a leadership role in their own lives.

Celebrating a successful camp   Philippines

---

[1] Armenia, Belize, Bulgaria, Cape Verde, Estonia, Kazakhstan, Kyrgyz Republic, Latvia, Lithuania, Macedonia, Madagascar, Moldova, Morocco, Namibia, Philippines, Poland, Romania, Russia, Slovakia, South Africa, and Uzbekistan.

[2] Excerpted from the Percy Amendment of 1974.

Each Camp GLOW reflects the unique characteristics and diversity of its local community. Drawing on the skills and talents of the organizers and the participants, as well as local needs and resources, many innovative adaptations of Camp GLOW have taken place. In this way Camp GLOW has been effective in promoting awareness among girls of other issues important to their lives and their communities. Here are just two examples:

• In the Philippines Volunteers and host-country nationals focused their camp on the interconnectedness of women and the environment.

• In Madagascar Camp GLOW served as a foundation for a peer education project to teach high school students about the transmission and prevention of HIV/AIDS.

The Future of Camp GLOW

As Camp GLOW continues to grow, there are challenges and a great deal of which to be proud. Many Peace Corps posts are considering how to make Camp GLOW more sustainable, how to best pass on lessons learned about Camp GLOW, and how to allow it to reach the greatest number of community members possible. In addition, organizers and campers are constantly seeking ways to spread the camp's message of empowerment, self-development, and gender equity.

Listening and learning   The Gambia

As in all Peace Corps project activities, Volunteers are expected to implement Camp GLOW in a way that builds sustainability beyond Peace Corps. One strategy is collaborating with local non-governmental organizations (NGOs) in the planning and implementation of Camp GLOW. For example, in Uzbekistan, local women are trained to gradually take over the organization and leadership of the camps and Volunteers in Latvia involve NGOs in their camp. Lastly, the role of Junior Counselor and Junior Director not only builds sustainability of the activity, but also reinforces the girls' leadership skills.

In addition to ensuring financial sustainability, Volunteers involved in Camp GLOW (and other girls' leadership camps) have developed innovative ways to ensure that the campers apply what they learned at the camp when they return home. In Poland, for example, past participants have started Clubs GLOW at local high schools and have created a girls' magazine called "Iron Daisies." One of the expected outcomes of a leadership camp in South Africa is that girls' leadership clubs are started in the communities where the participants live. Volunteers in Namibia held a series of GLOW workshops where the girls learned how to start and maintain girls' clubs and how take a more active part in their own education.

About this Handbook

Building on the successes of past camps, Peace Corps developed this publication to address the most common questions about Camp GLOW and share lessons learned from Volunteers who have organized past camps. This *Handbook* incorporates information from Camp GLOW country manuals, funding reports, Project Status Reports, Emails, and other sources of information. The publication will, hopefully, serve as a tool for Volunteers and host-country nationals who want to organize and host a Camp GLOW. Creativity and flexibility are keys to making Camp GLOW a success in your community and you are encouraged to adapt the ideas in this *Handbook* to your context.

Perhaps you will develop terminology that is culturally relevant for your Camp GLOW. For the purposes of this *Handbook*, however, we have used the following terms consistently throughout.

- **Counselor** refers to a Volunteer or host-country national who is a member of the organizing committee of Camp GLOW and involved in the planning and coordination of all camp activities.

- **Camper** refers to a female between the ages of 12-18 who attends Camp GLOW.

- **Junior counselor** is a high school student or recent graduate of high school. She has attended a previous Camp GLOW and shown exemplary leadership skills. The Camp GLOW organizing committee invites junior counselors to receive additional leadership training and attend Camp GLOW as part of the organizing committee. Some Camps GLOW refer to junior counselors as mentors.

You are wished great success in your efforts with Camp GLOW and encouraged to share your experience with other Volunteers and Peace Corps staff.

Teamwork in action   Guyana

CHAPTER 1: PLANNING

In this section of the *Handbook*, you will find a Camp GLOW timeline, ideas for organizing your leadership committee, brainstorming community needs, and establishing goals and objectives. Also, included in this chapter are suggestions for identifying partner organizations, tips for creating a budget, and questions to ask when looking for a campsite. All of these activities can lay the "groundwork" for your camp by creating a unified vision and sharing responsibilities among your camp organizers. In addition, having a plan and vision can aid your fundraising efforts and best use your community and human resources.

CAMP GLOW TIMELINE

Following is a timeline to assist Camp GLOW organizers. The timeline highlights the main topics covered in this manual. Many of the tasks listed below occur simultaneously and there is not a rigid order to follow. This timeline highlights the principle issues to consider in project planning for Camp GLOW. Each organizing committee is encouraged to adapt and add details to this timeline to make it more relevant to their own experience.

This timeline is based on information taken from Volunteer and staff reports submitted after Camp GLOW activities in the Philippines (2000), Romania (1999 and 2000), and Poland (1998 and 1999); and from *Beyond the Classroom: Empowering Girls Idea Book*, Peace Corps. Washington, D.C.: Information and Collection Exchange, Publication No. M0080, February 2000.

You may want to check off each item as it is completed.

CAMP GLOW TIMELINE

Six to Nine Months in Advance

☐ Establish organizing committee of camp counselors (e.g., Volunteers and nationals including people who can help get local support, transportation, camp location) See Chapters One and Three.

☐ Begin reading camp materials.

☐ Discuss goals for Camp GLOW. See Chapter One.

☐ Identify partner organizations and individuals to work with Volunteers (e.g., teachers, local NGOs). See Chapter One.

☐ Do a needs assessment. See Chapter One.

☐ Investigate possible funding sources and begin grant application process (e.g., local support, Peace Corps, family and friends). See Chapter Two.

Four to Five Months in Advance

☐ Determine size of the camp and decide on approximate dates.

☐ Determine eligibility (e.g., identifying campers and counselors). See Chapter Two.

☐ Investigate possible camp locations and conference centers. See Chapter One.

☐ Create Budget. See Chapter One.

☐ Develop schedule, camper selection process, and supply lists. (Some materials might take time to get, so allow time for ordering and shipment.)

☐ Invite guest speakers to participate and confirm contracts with partner organization.

☐ Determine who your junior counselors will be (e.g., their role, training needed). See Chapter Two.

Two to Three Months in Advance

☐ Conduct informational meetings with potential campers to tell them about Camp GLOW. See Chapter Two.

☐ Hold essay competition or mail out letter to teachers requesting nominations for campers. See Chapter Two and Appendix E for an Application Form.

☐ Evaluate Camp GLOW applications, select campers. See Chapter Two and Appendix E.

☐ Mail out acceptance, wait-list, and non-acceptance letters. See Appendix E for sample letters.

☐ Investigate any rules particular to your campsite or country (e.g., vaccination cards, on-site nurse, and insurance). See Chapter One.

☐ Hold training for junior counselors. See Chapter Two.

Camp GLOW Timeline – Page 1 of 3

One Month in Advance

☐ Reconfirm all speakers.

☐ Reconfirm all event plans (food, lodging, and transportation).

☐ Formulate a back-up plan for problems you can anticipate such as rainy days, or a camper going home early. See Chapter Three.

☐ Have orientation meetings for all the campers in their towns. See Chapter Two.

☐ Invite parents.

☐ Pass out packing lists, permission slips, and any other documents that parents or other officials must sign for the camp.

One Week in Advance

☐ Have a meeting of the counselors and junior counselors to review the schedule. See Chapter Three.

☐ Do you have everything that you need for every activity?

☐ Is every minute of the schedule planned?

☐ Try to get some sleep.

☐ Review supply list. Have you remembered everything? See Chapter Two.

☐ Reconfirm campsite, speakers, food, and transportation. See Chapter Three.

The First Day of Camp

☐ Send a few counselors up to the camp early to greet the campsite managers, arrange meeting spaces, label dorm rooms or cabins, and set up a table with nametags.

☐ Take some time at night to get to know the other counselors if you are together for the first time.

☐ Relax and have fun, Camp GLOW is finally happening!

During the Camp

☐ Follow schedule as planned.

☐ Take pictures and/or videotape.

☐ Hold daily or weekly check-in meetings with counselors to review day's highlights, revise agenda, and trouble shoot.

After the Camp

- [ ] Celebrate! See Chapter Five.

- [ ] Tabulate camp evaluations. See Chapter Five.

- [ ] Send thank-you notes to donors and all others who helped to make Camp GLOW a success. See Chapter Five.

- [ ] Complete grant reports. See Chapter Five.

- [ ] Evaluate the camp. See Chapter Five.

- [ ] Plan a time to discuss. See Chapter Five.

  - [ ] Camp GLOW evaluations from campers with other counselors

  - [ ] What the counselors thought of the camp

  - [ ] Record lessons learned and a list of resources. Distribute this to Peace Corps Program Officers and the WID/GAD office. (This will help Volunteers in future groups organize their Camp GLOW.)

- [ ] Plan follow-up activities with the campers. See Chapter Six.

- [ ] Do follow-up with parents or guardians. (Maybe the parents/guardians/family would enjoy a camper-led workshop of one of the most successful activities at your camp, so that they can get a flavor of what happened.) See Chapter Six.

- [ ] Translate materials as necessary. For example, if future Camp GLOW clubs or leadership workshops are going to focus on including people that do not speak English, you may want to consider creating a short guide to Camp GLOW in local languages to help promote sustainability. See Chapter Six.

Sharing in a safe environment   Namibia

LEADERSHIP WITHIN THE ORGANIZING COMMITTEE

Volunteers have noted that it is important to define the roles and responsibilities of counselors within the "organizing committee." The organizing committee should reflect your local community. Consider including host-country nationals on the organizing committee such as campers, junior counselors, teachers, NGO representatives, etc. Some camps choose to name a director, others do not. (In Ukraine, Camp GLOW has a Project Director, a third year camper who works on planning and administration of the camp, as a way to transfer skills.)

Volunteers have defined the main areas of responsibilities as:

Scribe/Note-taker at all meetings

Responsibility: Writes down important ideas, organizational information and decisions, compiles meeting minutes, and distributes the notes to all the counselors.

Scheduler and Time-keeper

Responsibility: Develops schedule, confirms guest speakers, and posts schedule during camp. This person keeps things moving during camp.

Fundraiser

Responsibility: Tracks all funding requests, produces materials to distribute for fundraising efforts.

Camp Liaison

Responsibility: Researches and visits campsites, asks questions, makes sure campsite is paid, and reservation is confirmed. During the camp, this person speaks to the director about any issues that arise.

Rule Enforcer

Responsibility: Speaks to individual campers during the camp about any disciplinary issues and seeks the support and advice of the other counselors behind the scenes.

Supply Officer

Responsibility: Gathers all supplies before the camp and makes sure they are where they need to be during the camp.

Community Liaison

Responsibility: Publicizes camp in the community and issues special invitations as relevant; makes sure guest speakers are compensated for their participation; sends thank you notes to community members as needed.

Sanitation Engineer

Responsibility: Assigns cleaning tasks as relevant.

Transportation Officer

Responsibility: Establishes means of transport for campers to arrive at camp and makes sure campers have all necessary documentation to get discounts on public transportation.

NEEDS ASSESSMENT

Community development is often the most effective when it arises from the needs and desires of the local population. Including host-country nationals is a necessary step for getting ideas and insights for your Camp GLOW and building sustainability. Host-country nationals can draw on outside community resources and provide insights into the current challenges and opportunities for women and girls. In addition, having people share their past experiences of camp not only "breaks the ice," but can lead to the development of new ideas.

While planning Camp GLOW, organizers around the world from Belize to Latvia, Morocco to Uzbekistan have found it necessary to begin the Camp GLOW organizational process by identifying the needs of the campers within the context of their local communities (where they live, work and study). In addition, organizers have considered general attitudes and opportunities for women at the national level. These considerations have lead to goals for individual camps which reflect the needs and realities of the campers.

Brainstorming Community Needs

Once you have a team of Camp GLOW counselors or an organizing committee, if possible try to organize a face-to-face meeting with all involved. Many Volunteers have found Peace Corps events such as In-Service Training (IST) a good time to get together. Once you are gathered, select someone to facilitate a brainstorming session while another person writes down ideas on flip chart paper. Select a scribe to take notes to be distributed to counselors not present and to be used in the development of your camp materials. Defining the needs of the local community is not only a useful exercise to plan appropriate activities for your camp but also necessary for grant proposals and other funding requests.

Sample Brainstorming Questions:

- What general attitudes do you observe towards women in your community?

- What roles do women play inside and outside of the home?

- What opportunities exist for young women to develop their leadership skills, self-esteem, and confidence?

- Is there accurate health education for young women?

- What is the relationship between women and their environment?

- How can we make Camp GLOW sustainable?

- How can we present material in a culturally appropriate way?

- What are the common needs and interests of the young women in your community?

What is the Camp Culture?

For many people who grew up in the United States, "camp" means skills development (e.g., music, tennis) arts and crafts, songs, games and outdoor activities. In some Peace Corps countries, the concept of camp may be new or different from the way it is thought of in the United States. In the newly independent states (NIS) camp was thought of as a tool of the state to promote nationalism and pride in one's country. What does camp mean where you live?

In identifying the community needs, past participants in Camp GLOW have found it necessary to research the camp culture, and ideas and stigmas of camp in their respective countries. Volunteers have also explained Camp GLOW in creative ways. For example, in Romania and Poland camp is much different from camp in the United States. Campers have very little supervision and there are few, if any, set activities. Each day is spent at the local lake, river or nearby town and nights at the "disco" usually on the campgrounds. Consequently, the campers in these countries were surprised when they arrived at Camp GLOW with a fixed schedule that had each day full of activities. Counselors therefore suggested that, in the future, Camp GLOW should not only be described as a camp but also a leadership conference or workshop.

Thinking about Camp Culture

- What is the camp culture in your country?

- Can young women spend an entire week away from home at an overnight camp or is it best and most cost-effective to organize a day camp or even a series of workshops over several weeks?

- What steps are necessary to explain Camp GLOW to students, parents/guardians, and other community members?

ESTABLISHING GOALS AND OBJECTIVES

Once you have established the need for Camp GLOW decide what you want to accomplish during your camp. One of the best ways to do this is to talk about your experiences in your communities. What attitudes do you observe? What stereotypes exist? How do your colleagues and counterparts feel? What do they see as the greatest challenges facing women in the country where you are living?

Brainstorming your ideas and establishing formal goals will not only help you plan appropriate activities and present a uniform vision to the campers, it will also help you to market your camp to the greater community and donors.

Questions to consider as an organizing committee:

- How do we define leadership?

- What are our roles as coordinators of this camp?

- What are our expectations?

- What do we want the campers to take home from this camp?

- What are our goals and objectives? (See text box below for examples.)

- In what language will the camp be conducted (e.g., local language, other languages, English)?

CAMP GLOW ARMENIA GOALS AND OBJECTIVES

Goal

The goal of this camp is to organize and provide a sustainable camp for young Armenian women aged 15-20. The camp will offer these women information in the areas of leadership, career choices, women's health issues, and self-discovery. Overall, the camp will provide a safe atmosphere in which one-hundred young women can freely explore their personality, their chosen career field, and hopefully decide their future goals and direction.

Objectives

1. Provide a fun, safe, bonding atmosphere in the form of a camp in order to promote self-discovery and career development.

2. Obtain materials and recruit Armenian female presenters to speak in Armenian on the following topics: personality and self-exploration, women's health issues, women and relationships in Armenia, leadership, and career development.

3. Create a bond between the young female participants and cabin mentors, special speakers, and career fair representatives.

4. Conduct a career fair for the participants comprised of Armenian professional women representing both various fields and locations throughout Armenia.

5. Ensure camp sustainability by:

   - Working in collaboration with NGOs that address gender issues; and

   - Working with the chosen camp leaders during the camp and throughout the following year to organize further leadership camp(s).

IDENTIFYING PARTNERS

Identifying open, supportive people to be involved with your Camp GLOW goes hand-in-hand with assessing the community's needs and setting realistic goals. After the first Camp GLOW in Morocco, the evaluations from the campers showed that the most effective camp sessions included the personal stories of Moroccan women rising above obstacles to accomplish their goals. In the past, Camps GLOW have connected with community and national groups. Some past partners with whom Volunteers have collaborated:

- Educators, teachers, principals

- Doctors, nurses, community health workers

- Women's associations, for example, female university professors

- Local, national and international organizations such as the Girls Scouts, Outward Bound, Harbaek Foundation and the Soros Foundation/Open Society Foundation can be approached. Please see the "Fundraising" section of this *Handbook* in Chapter Two for more information.

- Local government offices

- Women doing innovative work such as starting NGOs to address community needs

- Women in politics

Working with partner organizations helps to ensure sustainability. Partners can also help you make sure that ideas are presented in a culturally appropriate way. In addition, working in partnership with local organizations and individuals empowers women to take leadership roles within their communities. In the Kyrgyz Republic, Volunteers trained local university students to serve as counselors, involving them from the beginning in the initial stages of organizing Camp GLOW. University GLOW Club members received training in developing a budget, writing grants, designing a schedule, and planning logistics. After the camp, Counselors learned about grant reporting and follow-up activities. Now these women are aiding high school students in organizing GLOW clubs in high schools and implementing additional camps.

> *Working at summer camps with Bulgarian teachers and students gave Volunteers a chance to communicate with Bulgarians in a more informal context and provided for intensive inter-cultural exchange of opinions and ideas.*

> **Excerpt from the fiscal year 2000 Project Status Report, Initiative Report: Girls' Education, Peace Corps/ Bulgaria**

CREATING A BUDGET

Before you fundraise or invite campers, you need to create a budget. See Appendices A and H (page 7 of 7) for a sample budget. Keep in mind that different donors and funding sources have different report requirements and restrictions in terms of what types of activities and materials they can fund.

IMPORTANT EXPENSES TO CONSIDER INCLUDING IN YOUR BUDGET

Activities during Camp

☐ Activity fees (For example, if you are going to a lake what is the price of admission?)

☐ Activity/art supplies

☐ Honorarium, lodging, meals, and travel expenses for guest speakers

☐ Session Materials (See "Supply list" Chapter Two)

Communication

☐ Telephone bills/phone cards (For example, if your organizing committee is in different towns, you should budget for long distance phone calls.)

☐ Internet time (if you need to pay to use the internet to Email the other members of your organizing committee)

Lodging

☐ Lodging (What does the campsite, conference center, or hotel cost per night per person? Are there group discounts or any other discounts?)

☐ Insurance (for example, travel or campsite insurance)

Material Production and Distribution

☐ Camper Manual production (for example, ink, paper, copying costs, translation into local language)

☐ Film developing (copies of pictures for campers and donors)

☐ Photocopies (for example, worksheets, letters to campers, health forms, camp contact information for parents, thank you letters, post-camp letters/newsletters, song sheets)

☐ Postage (for example, camp applications to evaluators, packing lists, acceptance, non-acceptance or wait-list letters, mailings of meeting notes to organizing committee, post-camp follow-up letter or newsletter)

☐ Computer time (Do you have to pay for this or can you consider access to a computer as an in-kind community donation?)

☐ Translation of materials (for example, permission slips, camp manuals, activity sheets)

Meals

☐ Food (How many meals will you eat together each day?)

☐ Snacks

Transportation

☐ Transportation to and from camp for campers

☐ Transportation for Camp GLOW organizing committee and any guest speakers

IDENTIFYING A CAMPSITE

Finding a campsite can be a daunting task for a Volunteer. Having a local community member participate in the process can be an enormous asset. The following are some questions compiled by Volunteers who have located campsites for Camp GLOW:

Questions to Ask:

- Is there a set schedule at the campsite?
- What is the meal schedule? (If there are no meals provided, are there cooking facilities we can use or a caterer we can hire?)
- Are there sport facilities?
- How many other camps will be sharing the campgrounds with us?
- What are their ages? (This can affect the girls.)
- What are their sexes?
- Are we required to participate in any activities with the other campers?
- Is there an indoor area if it rains?
- Does the camp provide bedding? If so, is there an additional fee?
- Is there laundry service?
- What are the rules at this camp? How does the camp staff view campers who smoke and drink during the camp? How are campers who break the rules disciplined? Who has final say in this policy?
- How many people to a room?
- Do all of the counselors need to stay together in one room?
- What is our access to bathrooms or latrines?
- Is there potable water on-site? If not, how will we transport it to the campsite?
- Is there a store nearby to buy snacks?
- What days and times do you want us to arrive and depart?
- Is there an outdoor area?
- Can we have campfires?
- What activities are available in the area? Are there places within walking distance to hike, swim, shop, or bowl?
- Where is the closest medical facility? What is the transportation to this facility?
- Is there a camp nurse or doctor? What hours does she work? Do we need to pay for her services? Do we need to provide her with any information?
- Will we have access to telephones? What is the cost for calls we make?
- Is there an emergency contact number that we can give to parents?
- Do cell phones work at the campsite?

Tip

Visit the camp as soon as you can and talk with the Camp Director. Explain to him/her the nature of Camp GLOW early on so that they will understand that this is a different kind of camp! Bring a native speaker with you to explain and to avoid misunderstandings!

CHAPTER 2: LOGISTICS

In this section of the *Handbook*, you will find tips for planning from past counselors, background information on past camps, and questions to ask while you are organizing Camp GLOW. Figuring out the logistics of Camp GLOW will take time and effort before the camp happens. During the camp, however, your efforts will pay off. The camp will flow from activity to activity without having to make decisions on the spot. Campers and counselors will already know what to do and when to do it. This will reduce stress on the organizing team and allow them to focus on the goals of the camp.

Planning logistics for Camp GLOW is unique because it is a chance to develop individual leadership skills and give the members of your organizing committee experience working as a team. Organizing logistics is also a chance to build ties to the community.

When logistics are thoroughly thought out, they should answer the questions: who, what, when, where and how? For example, when thinking about transportation on a bus, consider: Can you charter a special bus? What does the bus cost? Who will drive the bus? What time will the bus depart and arrive? How will campers get to the bus? Where does the bus go? Do you need to tip the driver? Do you need to provide overnight housing and meals for the driver?

TIPS FOR SMOOTH LOGISTICS

✔ Send parents all necessary emergency contact information.

✔ Consider how you are going to enforce the rules of your camp before it starts. Will you send campers who break a rule home immediately? If so, how will they get home? If not, what consequences will there be to breaking the rules?

✔ Encourage the girls not to bring cell phones. They can be very distracting to the flow of the camp and lead to other problems, such as visitors, if the camp facility is close to the home community.

✔ Ask an adult to have a cell phone at the camp or phone cards to make emergency calls home to parents or Peace Corps.

✔ If you are traveling to camp on a bus, keep an eye out for motion sickness. Many of the girls may not be used to traveling very long distances. Make sure you have plastic bags, water, and paper towels on the bus.

✔ Have a good start with your relationship with the Camp Director. Explain what you are doing from the beginning. Camp GLOW may not be like other camps in your country and they are going to wonder what is going on! (See the "Camp Culture" and "Identifying a Campsite" sections in Chapter One.)

✔ Homesickness will be a factor. Make sure the girls know that you are there for them and keep them busy!

✔ Be aware of the cultural context of menstruation. For example, in some countries, menstruating girls might not shower or participate in sports.

SUPPLIES

What supplies you need depends on where and when your Camp GLOW is happening. Here is a list based on Volunteers' suggestions. For a suggested camper packing list, please see Appendix C.

Session Materials

- Balloons
- Contact paper
- Crayons
- Crepe paper
- Envelopes
- Flipchart paper
- Glue sticks
- Heavy-duty tape
- Journals
- Magazines
- Markers
- Masking tape
- Nametags
- Pencils
- Pens
- Photocopies – think of what copies you need for the sessions you are leading
- Reams of paper
- Scissors – include on the packing list for campers
- Spray paint (for logos on Camp GLOW T-shirts)
- Yarn

Sports Equipment

- Beach balls
- Frisbees
- Hula hoops
- Jump ropes
- Soccer ball
- Whistle

Basic Needs

- Good pocket knife
- Toilet paper
- Water filter

House Wares

- Bedding (sheets, blankets, sleeping bags, pillows)
- Food
- Plates, cups and cutlery
- Pots and pans
- Towels

Medical Supplies

- Bug repellent
- Campers emergency release forms/ medical information
- Feminine hygiene products
- First Aid kits
- Sunscreen
- Plastic surgical gloves

Other

- Batteries
- Camera/film
- Garbage bags
- Tape player and tapes
- Alarm clocks
- Snacks for campers
- Extension cords

Craft Supplies

- Buckets
- Dye
- Embroidery floss for friendship bracelets
- Fabric paints
- Pipe cleaners
- Stamps and pads
- T-shirts

Prizes/Awards

- Camp GLOW certificates
- Dictionaries
- Hair clips
- Stickers

SELECTING CAMPERS, JUNIOR COUNSELORS AND COUNSELORS

Selecting Campers

Volunteers and their colleagues have found that Camp GLOW generates interest quickly among young people. Different groups of counselors have developed distinct ways of selecting campers. Below are some examples of different selection processes.

Camper Selection through an In-class Essay Contest

In Romania, counselors invited all female English students from grades 8-11 (ages 14-18) who had studied English at least three years to participate in essay contests. All potential campers came from the same towns as the camp counselors because one of their camp goals was to do follow-up activities.

1. First, camp counselors held information sessions where they presented camp goals and the basic rules. See Appendix D for a sample flyer advertising Camp GLOW.

2. Counselors held an in-class essay contest for all the girls who wanted to apply for the camp. The reason the contest was in-class was that the counselors did not want the girls to have help with their essays. See Appendix E for essay application, and essay-evaluation form.

3. Three Volunteers who did not know the applicants read the essays (to guarantee impartiality) and graded on content, ideas, and ability to communicate clearly. Counselors created a wait-list and communicated with all girls as to the status of their applications. See Appendix E for acceptance, non-acceptance and wait-list letters.

4. Once counselors established a final list of campers, there was a meeting in each town for the girls and their parents to get their packing lists, to pay their deposits, and to get all other information. See Appendix C for a packing list and Appendix F for a permission slip.)

Camper Selection through a Nomination by a Teacher

In Poland and Bulgaria, Volunteers sent a letter to English teachers asking them to choose a few female students (ages 13-19) from each class who were active in the classroom, cooperative, team-oriented and had a positive attitude. Counselors encouraged the teachers to use two essay questions to help them decide which potential campers to select. See Appendix G for letters.

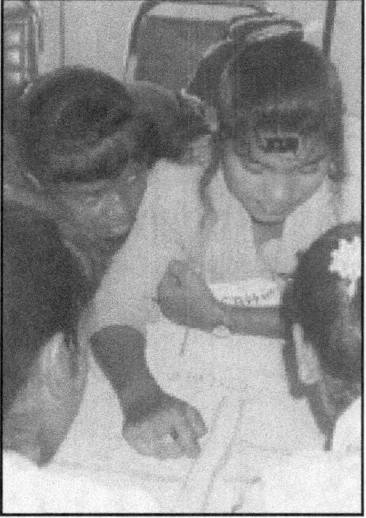

Camper Selection Based on Community Involvement

Since Camp GLOW in the Philippines that had an environmental focus, counselors selected campers (ages 13-19) based on their work in their own community. Some of the participants were members of youth conservation clubs or science clubs at their schools. Counselors interviewed potential campers or asked them to write an essay based on the question "What is one problem facing Filipina women today?" The camp content reflected the concerns outlined in the essays and during the interviews.

Working together   Guyana

Selecting Counselors

Every Camp GLOW has counselors or some form of leadership. When selecting your counselors it is important to select adults who want to be mentors and role models. People that are interested in working as a team, open to new ideas and share common goals often create the most responsive counselors. Following are some issues to consider when you select counselors.

Issues to consider:

- Proximity to and willingness to work with campers during and after Camp GLOW

- Openness to new ideas

- A demonstrated interest in issues promoted by Camp GLOW, for example, a commitment to the environment or community involvement on issues relating to women

- Language abilities (Can the counselor communicate with campers and other counselors?)

- Some Camps GLOW have included male Volunteers as counselors and have found it very successful. It is important for the campers to have positive male role models as part of their experience.

- Both American and host-country national counselors can provide additional dynamics to your camp as well as build sustainability.

Selecting Junior Counselors

A junior counselor is a person who has attended a previous Camp GLOW and shown exemplary leadership skills. Counselors usually nominate junior counselors for the position or invite all former campers to apply. If you are organizing a Camp GLOW, check with your Peace Corps country office or the WID/GAD Volunteer committee for a list of junior counselors. Utilizing junior counselors promotes sustainability of Camp GLOW, allows them to apply the knowledge and skills gained at the camp, and gives them unique leadership and mentoring possibilities.

Junior counselors are being incorporated into the Camp GLOW model all around the world. They are involved in all phases of planning and implementing the camps. In Bulgaria, one Volunteer serves as the Junior Counselor Coordinator. The role of the Coordinator is to ensure that the junior counselors understand their duties and are comfortable with their roles. Junior counselors have led fundraisers at their high schools for Camp GLOW, assisted with recruitment of applicants, petitioned local businesses for support, and have led Camp GLOW sessions.

In Romania, junior counselors from three different geographical regions received additional training at a two-day workshop. This prepared the junior counselors to assume leadership roles and actively participate in the Camp GLOW planning. In Slovakia, junior counselors are paired with regular counselors to assist with facilitation of sessions and provide explanations to small groups. For example, if you do a session on self-esteem you and the junior counselor decide exactly how the session will be organized, and you lead it together. In addition, junior counselors can lead free time activities, icebreakers, and games. In Bulgaria, a junior director is selected through an intensive interview process with all interested junior counselors.

See the box below for information on the topics presented at the Junior Counselor Training.

> ## Junior Counselor Training
> ## Romania
>
> ### Topics presented:
>
> **What is a GLOW mentor/junior counselor?**
>
> **Listening skills and confidentiality**
>
> **Sharing personal camp experiences**
>
> **Appreciating diversity**
>
> **Team-building and promoting self-esteem**
>
> **Conflict resolution**
>
> **Small group discussion**
> **Presentation of timeline for camp preparation**
> **Goal setting**

POTENTIAL RESOURCES

Here are some specific and general resources for organizing Camp GLOW, including, fundraising ideas, people and resources for the content of your camp.

People

Peace Corps staff, counterparts, teachers, principals and other Volunteers are all good sources of information. Ask your Program Managers/APCDs if previous Volunteers in other groups have left behind any information on Camp GLOW. See "Identifying Partner Organizations" in the previous section of the *Handbook* for more ideas on harnessing your "people power." It offers suggestions on different kinds of international, national, and grassroots organizations to contact.

Bringing together people of diverse backgrounds adds to the richness of Camp GLOW. For example, including teachers and principals in your organizing committee, consulting with them in a distinct advisory capacity; or inviting them as guest speakers can give you a window into the workings of the school system and formal education in your host country. Teachers and principals might have ideas for other community contacts and funding sources or know of campsites that provide discounts to students. Including mayors or other public officials in some capacity can get the community motivated and create opportunities for positive publicity. In addition, government officials may help to identify local funding sources whether they are private or public or help find camp facilities in the local area.

Also, using people from your local host community is a wonderful way to promote or encourage women in leadership roles.

Working with other Organizations

When working with non-governmental organizations, the organizing committee and the NGO staff and/or Volunteers should determine the role of the NGO within Camp GLOW. Sometimes the NGOs are included in all phases of the camp. During other camps, the organizing committee assigns out certain responsibilities to the NGO such as team-building or food services. Working with local NGOs provides opportunities for their professional development. In addition, it can build the capacity and confidence of the NGO staff by giving them the opportunities to work with counselors and campers.

Outward Bound

Outward Bound is an organization that employs professional experiential educators to lead team-building activities. Romanian camps have worked with Outward Bound Romania. Outward Bound has provided a team-building component that complemented the discussion topics during other sessions. To locate Outward Bound affiliates in your country, go to the Outward Bound International website at www.outwardbound.org and you will find a directory of Outward Bound schools and contact information for each country.

4-H International

The 4-H youth development program is a dynamic non-formal education program, which provides opportunities to learn life skills; gain knowledge while having fun; and make contributions in such areas as environmental education, community service, and current youth issues. The program is dedicated to providing opportunities for young people to develop positive self-esteem, leadership and management skills, effective communication skills, a solid sense of personal responsibility, and the ability to make sound decisions. For more information go to http://www.nmsu.edu/~state4h/about4h.html

Junior Achievement

Junior Achievement International (JAI) is a not-for-profit organization dedicated to providing high quality business and economic education courses for youth. JAI offers more than 20 different business and economic education courses for all age groups from kindergarten to young adults. JAI and the Peace Corps work together to help interested countries develop sustainable economic education programs through cooperation, planning, programming, training, management assistance, and other areas. For more information on JAI and member countries, go to their website at www.jaintl.org.

> *The [Camp GLOW] facilitators learned how to examine their own roles, gained facilitation skills in preparing and presenting interactive workshop curricula, and gained an enormous amount of self-esteem and satisfaction by becoming role models for young women within their own community. This is very important as the facilitators are all college educated young women who are currently unemployed due to the extreme scarcity of work available for the population in general and particularly women as men are prioritized for employment as heads of household. This experience gave the facilitators a sense of self worth and acknowledged the value of their skills.*
>
> **Excerpt from a report on Camp GLOW Morocco, July 2000**

Ideas for Fundraising

Fundraising is a skill that develops over time with practice. In the United States, activities such as students selling candy bars or holding car washes for schools or special projects are common. At Peace Corps posts, activities such as these may be less popular. In order to sustain Camp GLOW over the long-term, the focus of fundraising efforts should be at the local level. Any skills that you can transfer to local counterparts in the area of fundraising are invaluable. When organizing fundraising campaigns, focus on planning your steps and strategies, creating detailed information (flyers, brochures, contracts for sponsors to sign) and preparing verbal summaries that can give individuals more confidence when they are speaking about Camp GLOW in public.

- Funding for a first Camp GLOW in any given country may be available from The Center for Field Assistance and Applied Research at Peace Corps/Washington. Program Managers/APCDs make Center requests. Contact your Program Manager/APCD for more information.

- Volunteers cannot directly solicit funds in writing in the name of Peace Corps to organizations based outside their country of service. Volunteers can however, aid their colleagues in preparing to visit local businesses to ask for donations of materials or money. Preparing a "pitch" is a good skills-building activity to do with your junior counselors or other colleagues. If you are working with an NGO, school or another organization, you may accompany your colleagues on a fundraising visit. Please contact your in-country Peace Corps Partnership Coordinator (this is an in-country Peace Corps staff person) for more information on this topic.

- Investigate if the local government has any special funds for girls' educational activities. In Uzbekistan, the local government sponsored a Camp GLOW. Camp GLOW organizers approached government officials in November for a summer camp, which gave government officials time to find the funds from the local budget.

- The U.S. Embassy may provide both material support and in-kind donations. Volunteers in Poland and Romania have used Democracy Funds from the U.S. Embassy for several of their Camps GLOW. Volunteers incorporated sessions during the camp such as holding a mock election and creating GLOW party platforms, which focused on democracy and leadership skills. See Chapter Three "Activities for Implementation" and Chapter Four "Applications of Camp GLOW" of this *Handbook* for more information. Please note that posts can only accept up to $5,000 of private sector funds (such as the Democracy or Self-Help Fund) directly and that these are "gifts" meaning that there are no stipulations or reporting requirements.

- There may be grant opportunities with international donors with offices in your country, such as the Soros Foundation/Open Society, National Endowment for Democracy, World Learning, FAWE (Forum for African Women Educationalists), UNICEF, UNIFEM, private expatriate corporations, and others. If you are working in partnership with a local NGO, school or organization, that organization may be able to solicit funds for Camp GLOW. If you are not working with an organization that has "official status" and can apply for these funds, then you should ask your Peace Corps Partnership Program in-country coordinator to contact the PCPP specialist in Washington to see if you can approach these organizations. Please note, Volunteers should never approach any international governmental organization such as USAID, World Bank, and others without first contacting their PCPP coordinator who will then contact their PCPP specialist. These foundations and intergovernmental organizations can be good resources for guest speakers and information if not for funds. Peace Corps staff may know of contacts at these organizations. See Appendix H for sample grants and a grant report.

- The Peace Corps Partnership Program (PCPP) supports activities that promote leadership and empowerment of women and girls. For more information, contact your Program Manager/APCD or the PCPP coordinator in your country. (See Appendix H for sample grants and a grant report. Please note that reporting guidelines and formats may change. Check with the PCPP coordinator at post for the most recent format for grant proposals.)

- Associations of Returned Peace Corps Volunteers (RPCVs) have supported past camps through in-kind donations (e.g., tie-dye, prizes or s'mores supplies — graham crackers, chocolate and marshmallows). In-kind donations are sent directly from RPCV groups to Volunteers. For funding, you can list RPCV groups as referrals if you are requesting funds from the Peace Corps Partnership Program (PCPP). Otherwise, contact the Office of Private Sector Cooperation and International Volunteerism (OSPC&IV) at Peace Corps/Washington and they will approach the group on your behalf.

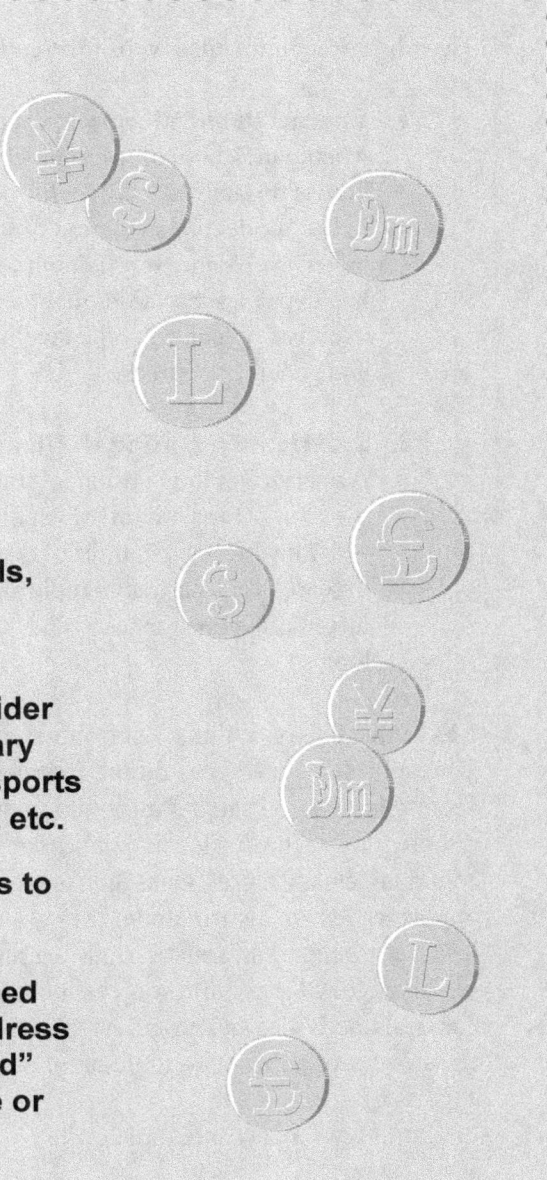

Tips
on
FUNDRAISING
from
Camp GLOW Organizers

- Try to get as many community donations as possible for materials, food, lodging or other in-kind donations.

- If materials are hard to find, consider having participants bring necessary items such as notebooks, pens, sports equipment, music, sleeping bags, etc.

- During the camp, ask the campers to write special thank-you notes to sponsors, donors, kitchen staff, drivers and anyone else who helped with the camp. Have campers address them to "Dear Camp GLOW Friend" and you can use them for anyone or make copies as necessary.

SOURCES OF INFORMATION

Internet

The Internet is a great source of information for fundraising ideas, health issues, and leadership. Some examples of relevant resources include:

- **Girls' Pipeline to Power** is an organization that helps girls become community activists; gives girls leadership opportunities; and makes sure that girls have access to information about politics. They have an impressive guide called *Take Action! Take Action!* which defines leadership skills, goal setting, and how to get involved in the political process in a concise and fun manner. It is available on the internet and can be downloaded with Adobe Acrobat. The Girls' Pipeline to Power website also has links to many useful Internet sites relating to leadership. Contact Information: Girls' Pipeline to Power, c/o Patriots' Trail Girl Scout Council, 95 Berkley Street, Boston, MA 02116, USA, Email: girlspipeline@girlspipeline.org, website: www.girlspipeline.org.

- Two highly recommended website directories on teen health are:

  1. **Internet Public Library** is a public service organization coordinated by the University of Michigan School of Information. This site lists resources and evaluates them for quality. To use this site to access information on teen health, go to their website at www.ipl.org. In the "collections" section of the web page, click on the teen icon. You will transfer to "teen" web page, scroll down to the health link and click on it. Once you reach the teen health page, subsections include: body image and eating disorders, disease and disorders, exercise, hygiene, mental health, nutrition, puberty, body changes, sex, substance abuse, and general resources.

  2. **SAMHSA's National Clearinghouse for Alcohol and Drug Information** is a service of the Substance Abuse and Mental Health Services Administration, a part of the U.S. Department of Health and Human Services. Their website address is: www.health.org. Features of this site include alcohol and drug fact sheets and the ability to search for a particular topic and select your audience. For example, you can search for information on "tobacco" and "teens." This site also has "Tips for Teens" on a variety of topics.

- **EE-Link**, This site links Environmental Education (EE) resources on the Internet. From this site, you can get information on resources for EE professionals, publications, communities, and professional development opportunities. It also includes EE grant resources, general information, and a grant search page. Classroom resources include materials, activities and programs for K-12 classrooms organized by topic area. The address is:
  http://www.nceet.snre.umich.edu/.

Publications

- *New Moon: The Magazine for Girls and Their Dreams*, New Moon Publishing, Inc.
  New Moon is an international magazine for girls who want to express their ideas and dreams. Girls ages eight to 14 from all over the world edit or contribute to the magazine. *New Moon* celebrates girls, explores the passage from girl to woman, and builds healthy resistance to gender inequities. Subscriptions available by accessing the New Moon website: www.newmoon.org.

- *The Exchange: Peace Corps' Women in Development Newsletter.*
  The Exchange is published quarterly by Women in Development, The Center for Field Assistance and Applied Research, Peace Corps/ Washington, DC and distributed to all Volunteers and Trainees. Each issue contains the success stories, project results, photos, and commentary from Peace Corps Volunteers involved in Women in Development and Gender and Development projects around the world. To contribute to this publication, please contact: Editor, The Exchange, Women in Development/Gender and Development, Peace Corps, 1111 20th Street NW, Washington, DC, 20526 USA.

- *The Girls' Guide to Life: How to Take Charge of the Issues that Affect You*. Catherine Dee (Author), Cynthia Jabar (Illustrator), Carol Palmer (Photographer), Little Brown & Co., ISBN: 0316179523
  The Girls Guide is a combination of personal stories and information covering topics such as self-esteem, cultural stereotypes, political awareness and sexual harassment.

Materials Available through Peace Corps' Information Collection and Exchange (ICE)

The Peace Corps Information Collection and Exchange (ICE) is a central technical information resource for Peace Corps staff and Volunteers to use during their service. ICE specializes in providing Peace Corps Volunteers and staff with the most relevant, up-to-date technical materials available in all program areas. See your Resource Manager or Program Manager/APCD to order materials from ICE.

The following resources, though not all specifically materials for girls' leadership, promote participatory practices and inclusion of both females and males. In addition, many of these resources can be used to enhance linkages between schools and communities using a community content-based instruction approach.

- **Another Point of View: A Manual on Gender Analysis Training for Grassroots Workers (Training Manual)**. A. Rani Parker. UNIFEM. 1993. (ICE WD108)
  Workshop and training manual focusing on gender issues in development. Specifically relevant to the experience of community-based development workers. Helpful in the design and implementation of gender-sensitive development programs at the grassroots level.

- ***Beyond The Classroom: Empowering Girls Idea Book**. Peace Corps. 2000 (ICE M0080)
  Dreaming, discovering, and growing is a life-long process. Volunteers can provide opportunities and serve as catalysts for this growth. Whether interacting with young women through schools, in communities, or in day-to-day exchanges, Volunteers have the potential to help girls change their

lives for the better. This booklet provides a collection of ideas and activities from Volunteers around the world to be used as a resource in the valuable work of empowering young women.

- **Children's Participation: From Tokenism to Citizenship**. Roger A. Hart. UNICEF International Child Development Centre. 1992. (ICE YD006)
  Describes as a ladder the different levels at which children have participated in decision-making, from simply making an appearance to actually initiating projects and sharing responsibilities with adults. Describes the British experience of children's participation through the schools in community research and development and children in developing countries taking charge of their lives.

- ***Choices: A Teen Woman's Journal for Self-Awareness and Personal Planning**. Mindy Bingham, Kathleen Peters (Editor), Barbara Green (Editor), Advocacy Press, 1983. (ICE WD135)
  Choices provides stories, activities, and suggestions on what it is like to be a girl and what expectations, values, and life options are determined by society and culture and, therefore, can be changed. This book provides a variety of exercises and activities for girls to do alone or in groups to better understand themselves, their aspirations and their potential. This book has been the basis of many Peace Corps activities such as Camp GLOW.

- ***Choose a Future! Issues and Options for Adolescent Boys** (ICE YD032). This manual is designed to foster self-respect, self-esteem, and supportive peer relationships; expand skills in analysis, decision-making, problem solving, and negotiating; and increase access to resources among young boys. In addition, boys explore gender-equitable approaches to family life and other socio-cultural issues and examine real issues in their lives — marriage, health, family relations, conflict resolution, education, work, legal status, and community involvement — and options for dealing with these issues.

- ***Choose a Future: Issues and Options for Adolescent Girls**. CEDPA Publications. 1996. (ICE WD127)
  Program guide for facilitators and trainers working with girls ages 12-20. Brings together ideas and activities to help adolescent girls learn about and deal with issues they face, including self-esteem problems, reproductive issues, decision-making skills, community involvement, and many more.

- **Gender and Development Training/ Girls' Education Manual**. Peace Corps. 1998. (ICE M0054)
  Product of the Gender and Development Training Initiative, which seeks to institutionalize the consideration of gender issues throughout Peace Corps. Contains eight booklets on gender and development training, which provide background and development of projects; training designs for various participants; session plans and handouts; and insights from the field. Contains four booklets on Girls' Education, including programming, training, and activities.

- **Leadership Development: A Handbook from YouthBuild USA and the Youth Action Program**. Dorothy Stoneman and John Bell, YouthBuild USA. 1993. (ICE YD008)
  A handbook based on ten years of experience building the Youth Action Program (YAP) of the East Harlem Block Schools. Contains background information on the accomplishments of the YAP program and is organized around the seven essential elements of leadership development: 1) counteracting the effects of oppression; 2) nurturing personal development; 3) teaching leadership skills; 4) providing the experience of success; 5) educating about the world; 6) resolving personal hang-ups and correcting academic deficiencies; and 7) organizing to have impact on the world.

Having fun and building confidence   Bulgaria

- **Life Planning Education**. The Center for Population Options. 1995. (ICE YD004)
  Comprehensive manual to prepare teenagers for the world of work and parenthood. Available in Spanish (ICE YD007).

- **Life Skills Manual**. Peace Corps. 2000 (ICE M0061)
  Addresses the important related issues of empowering girls and new values for boys. A behavior change approach that concentrates on the development of the skills needed for life, such as communication, decision-making, thinking, managing emotions, assertiveness, self-esteem building, resisting peer pressure, and relationship skills. The life skills program moves beyond providing information to the development of the whole individual so that the person will have the skills to make use of all types of information, whether it be related to HIV/AIDS, STDs, family decision-making, safe motherhood, other health issues, and any related data.

- **Navamaga: Training Activities for Group Building, Health and Income Generation**. Dian Svendsen and Sujatha Wijetillek. UNIFEM/Peace Corps. 1983. (ICE WD006)
  Handbook created by Sri Lankan rural development practitioners for grassroots development workers. It can be used as a tool to help villagers identify health and nutrition problems, increase their leadership skills and decision-making capabilities, and plan and implement small-scale projects to improve family nutrition and health and to increase family income. Available in Spanish (ICE WD071).

- ***The New Our Bodies, Ourselves: A Book by and for Women**. Jane Pincus and Wendy Sanford, Editors. (Simon and Schuster, Inc.) 1992. (ICE HE123)
  An updated and expanded version of the 1984 edition. Information on women's health. Subjects encompass sexuality, common medical and health problems, social diseases, decision-making, childbearing, abortion and parenthood.

- **PACA: Participatory Analysis for Community Action**. Peace Corps. 1996. (ICE M0053) Provides participatory methodology and techniques for working with communities. Includes tools that promote the inclusion of representative voices in a community in Peace Corps project planning and implementation. PACA is a step in institutionalizing the inclusion of women in all Peace Corps project development, monitoring, and implementation.

* Denotes resources used by Volunteers organizing Camp GLOW in the past.

New friends and role models   Bulgaria

CHAPTER 3: ACTIVITIES FOR IMPLEMENTATION

In this chapter of the **Handbook**, you will find tips for developing a schedule and a host of different ideas for activities to aid you in planning the content of your camp. Activities vary from team-building games to how to keep track of campers. While planning Camp GLOW the organizing committee should consider what type of activities are necessary to meet its goals. Camps GLOW have offered a mixture of daily informative, recreational, and developmental activities for the campers. This variety creates a fun and open atmosphere where each camper has a chance to display her strengths.

DEVELOPING A SCHEDULE

Developing a schedule lies at the core of camp planning and successful implementation of activities. A complete or master schedule should include: the start and conclusion of every activity (with time for breaks and transitions), an assigned leader/facilitator, the location of the activity and any materials needed. This planning helps avoid confusion, allows the day to flow from one activity to the next, and creates an atmosphere where both the counselors and campers can enjoy and learn from one another. See Appendix B for sample camp schedules.

Developing a camp schedule can be time consuming but necessary! When discussing the camp schedule refer to your needs assessment. Use this as a starting point in developing your sessions and schedule. There are many resources available to aid you in developing your camp schedule and Camp GLOW curriculum. One resource is the book **Choices: A Teen Woman's Journal for Self-awareness and Personal Planning**. Choices, the basis for the original Camp GLOW curriculum, is available through ICE (ICE WD135). For a list of additional ideas and resources, please see the "Potential Resources" section in Chapter Two and the "Activities for Implementation" section in Chapter Three of this **Handbook**. As you await your resources, you can begin planning your curriculum by learning what other camps have done. Camps GLOW usually have some of the following elements:

Tips
for Scheduling

- Determine (before camp starts):
  – How will you keep track of campers at all times?
  – How will you divide them up into groups for sessions?
  – Where will they sleep? Where will you sleep?
  – Decide which counselor will lead what group.
  – Assign night duty among counselors.

- While planning sessions and activities, remember to include a rainy day backup plan for each day.

- Post the daily schedule in the general meeting area so all participants can see it; it makes the campers less anxious.

Camp Planning Elements

Morning Sessions

Topics:

- Attitudes and stereotypes
- Self-esteem and values
- Goal setting
- Decision-making
- Conflict resolution
- Domestic violence
- Women's health issues
- Community service

Type of activities: small and large group discussions, role-plays, and worksheets

Rationale: Often, campers have more energy in the morning, therefore this is a good time to introduce concepts and invite guest speakers.

Afternoon Sessions

Topics:

- Team-building
- Artistic expression
- Health
- Democracy building
- Sports

Type of activities: icebreakers, games and low ropes course activities in small groups with experiential educator, bracelet making, kick-boxing, hiking, journaling, nutrition, and body image talks, yoga, GLOW Olympics, and environmental scavenger hunt.

Rationale: Energy level in the afternoons is usually lower than the mornings. This is a good time to plan more active sessions.

> *We feel that the amount of work that we put into our schedule before the camp paid off during the camp because we had an environment where everyone knew what was going on, where we should be, and who was in charge of each particular activity.*
>
> **Camp Counselor,
> Romania Camp GLOW 1999**

Evening sessions

Topics:

- Group bonding
- Creativity
- Relaxation

Type of activities: cabin cheer contests, talent shows, campfire songs, night hikes, discussions on stress, relaxation, and healthy relationships.

ACTIVITIES

The following is a list of some "tried and true" activities utilized during Camp GLOW. We hope that together with the "Potential Resources" section of the *Handbook*, it can help you get started on planning camp activities. In addition to the activities listed below, consult *Choices: A Teen Woman's Journal for Self-awareness and Personal Planning* and the "Potential Resources" section of the *Handbook* for additional ideas on developing your curriculum.

Part One: Management Activities

Name Tags

Purpose/Desired Outcome: Make it easy for everyone to learn names.

Pass out nametags with each camper's full name and room/cabin number on the back. On the front have each girl write her name or nickname. Require the campers and counselors to wear their nametags at all times. (Good quality nametags will last the whole camp.)

Night Duties

Purpose/Desired Outcome: Distribute late-night responsibilities among all counselors.

Give each GLOW Counselor a night to be "on duty." Responsibilities include checking to make sure the campers are in their rooms and quiet at "Lights Out." Additional responsibilities for the counselor "on duty" may include waking the girls up in time for breakfast and dealing with any problems that came up in the night, such as a sick camper.

Lights Out

Purpose/Desired Outcome: Help campers respect the "lights out" rule while making it fun. Campers' getting enough sleep affects their ability to participate in the next day's activities. One way to encourage "lights out" is to give a prize to the room(s) that is quiet with lights out at the scheduled time. The next morning have the counselor who was on duty the night before make a presentation awarding a prize for the campers that were in the quiet rooms. Camp GLOW Romania 1999 used butterfly hair clips. By the end of camp, everyone had won hair clips, and the counselors had five rooms out of six win the prize on the last night of camp. Positive reinforcement was a good way to make sure campers and counselors got much needed sleep.

Morning Announcements and Quote

Purpose/Desired Outcome: Start each morning in a fun and inspirational way.

Each morning pass out prizes or give praise to the room(s) that was quiet at "Lights Out" the night before. Give campers and counselors the opportunity to make announcements. End the morning announcements with an inspirational quotation read by a counselor or a camper.

Rule Development Exercise

Purpose/Desired Outcome: Have campers take ownership of the rules and understand why they are necessary.

1. As an entire group, have two counselors lead a brainstorming discussion on camp rules. Tell the campers that they are going to create the rules for camp and then you are all going to live by them. Encourage the campers to create rules that they were willing to follow and to speak up against rules that they think are unfair.

2. One counselor facilitates the discussion and the other writes the proposed rules on a piece of flipchart paper.

3. Then, as counselors, when the campers finish, add your own rules if they were not already mentioned (from your previously prepared list) and discuss them. (You may find that the campers' rules are more comprehensive and stricter than your own).

4. Confirm that everyone understands and accepts the rules.

5. Post the rules on the wall so they are accessible to every camper.

Camp GLOW is a drug-free environment. Nicotine, alcohol and other drugs are not permitted. Before the camp starts, you and the counselors need to consider how you will communicate and enforce these policies with campers, counselors and junior counselors. Consider that this is a leadership camp. All the campers are representing their communities and acting as role models. What would it mean if certain campers had their first drink or cigarette during Camp GLOW? One way to make sure that the campers understand the ramifications of abusing alcohol, cigarettes, and drugs during the camp is to make the campers sign a copy of a pledge stating that the camp is a smoking, drug, and alcohol free camp. State in the pledge what will happen if the campers break these rules. Translate this pledge into the local language and make sure the parents or guardians receive a copy of it so they understand if their camper is sent home. For an example of a camper's pledge, see Appendices E and F.

Learning to lead   Bulgaria

Part Two: Opening Activities

Affirmation Wall

Purpose: Team-building, creative expression and fun.

Desired Outcome: Positive reinforcement, increased self-confidence.

This was one of the most highly rated activities at Camps GLOW Romania. In a public place at your campsite hang large sheets of white paper. Divide it up into "puzzle" shaped pieces and have each camper and counselor write her name on a piece. Tell the campers that this affirmation wall is a way to express positive thoughts about others at camp. Leave a package of markers out near the wall. Encourage campers and counselors to write anonymous or signed messages. Stress that only positive messages are allowed. Messages will range from "I like your hair" or "Thanks for your insight in our discussion group" to "You are the best friend, I've ever had!" At the end of the camp, give each camper her puzzle-piece to take home.

Bead Bracelets

Purpose: Ice Breaker.

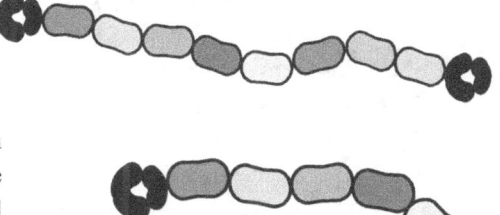

Desired Outcome: Meet new people.

Divide the campers up into groups. Give each group only one specific bead color. Tell the campers that their task is to make multi-colored bracelets. The way to get beads of many colors is to trade beads and personal information with campers from each group. In Morocco, this activity was very effective and without realizing it, the girls began to make new friends.

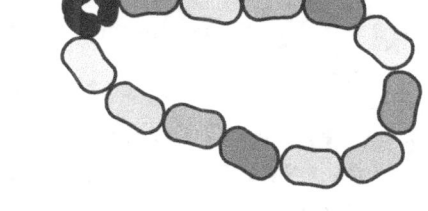

Part Three: Activities for Special Purposes
Confidence, Skills, Teamwork and Trust

Camera

Purpose: Teamwork.

Desired Outcome: Meet and work with new people.

Break the group up into pairs. One person in each pair should put on a blindfold - this person is the camera. The other partner is the photographer and should lead the camera around, occasionally stopping at something picturesque. The photographer should place the camera directly in front of what she wants the camera to see. At this point, the photographer should tap the camera on the shoulder and this person is allowed to peek from underneath the blindfold, but only for a second, imitating a camera taking a photo. Take several photos and then reverse the roles. After everyone has had the chance to be the camera, share descriptions of the photos as a group. Or if time allows, have everyone write a description and/or draw a picture of the photos and share in the big group.

Community Service: Putting Leadership into Action

Purpose: To learn what community service is and to design one specific community service project.

Desired Outcome: Campers will design a realistic community service project that they can carryout in their local communities.

Part I - Brainstorming

1. Ask the campers the following questions (Have a scribe write down the ideas on big paper during the discussion):

    *   What are some examples of communities? (e.g., family, church, school, town, Europe, world)

    *   What are some characteristics of a community? What makes a community a community? (e.g, common needs and interests, respect, a population, set of governing rules)

    *   Do you think that we have formed a community this week at GLOW? Why?

2. Show campers community maps drawn by counselors. They do not have to be literal maps of the community but can be representations through symbols such as a town represented as a flower with different petals.

3. Explain what community assets are — positive characteristics, aspects that benefit our communities.

4. Have groups of campers draw community maps. Divide campers up by town, not by discussion group. Pass out magic markers (every color but black) pens and big paper. Draw a map of the community. Be creative. Think out of the box!

Understanding communication through mapping   Guyana

5. Next, have the campers present their maps to the other groups.

6. Show counselor-drawn community maps again. Now add community problems, issues and challenges to community map in black. Explain that no community is perfect. Have groups add the problems, issues, and challenges to their maps and share them with the large group.

Valuing diverse opinions   Bulgaria

Part II – Discussion

1. What did the maps have in common? How does your community affect your self-esteem? Your values?

2. What was the point in making these maps? To remind ourselves of the many assets in our community and to learn about our problems.

3. Talk about community service. What is community service?

- Talk about "ripple effect" like throwing a stone into the water and having the rings spread across a pond. If we do something positive for our community, it can have a positive impact on our world just as doing something negative has an impact on our world. Example: If you throw a piece of trash in a river; it will make the river look ugly; kill the fish; people won't have anything to eat; pollute the drinking water etc.

- Give an example of some volunteer work that you have done. Use the format from the goal setting and achieving session on page 29. Answer the questions who, when, what, where, why and how and list the positive and negative outcomes. Stress the fact that the positives outweigh the negatives.

4. Ask the group – Why do community service? What can you learn from community service?

Part III – Develop a Plan of Action

1. In your groups, choose one issue, problem, or challenge to work on in your community over the next year.

   - Use the format that you have learned in the goal setting session (for more information see the goal setting activity in Chapter Three of this *Handbook*).

   - Example, do this in the big group together

     Mission Statement: Over the next year we will teach fourth graders about the dangers of smoking.

     Answer the questions who, what, when where, why, how, list the positive and negative outcomes, and draw a time line.

2. Have the groups present their action plans to the whole group.

   Resources for Community Mapping sessions:
   - *Promoting Powerful People*, Peace Corps, 2000. (ICE T0104)
   - *Gender and Development Training/Girls' Education Manual*, Peace Corps, 1997. (M0054 – Available only from your In-country Resource Center).

Democracy in Action or 'GLOWacracy'

Purpose: Teach campers about democracy in a fun and interactive way.

Desired outcomes: Planning for future GLOW activities, greater comfort with public speaking, democratic processes, and teamwork.

Part I – Preparation

1. Tell the campers they are going to choose a movie to watch tonight. Write three movies on the board. They must choose one of the three.

   - Anarchy exists when everyone is shouting out which movie she wants to see. Write "anarchy" on the board.

   - A dictatorship exists when one person makes all of the decisions without consulting the others. Tell one camper that she is the leader and ask her to choose a movie and that is the movie they will watch. Write "dictatorship" on the board.

   - Finally, hold a democratic election where everyone raises her hand to vote for one of the three movies listed. Write "democracy" on the board.

2. Allow every girl to name an influential woman in the world who they would like to see as President and state why. Vote on the president by raising hands.

3. Explain, what is democracy?

4. Explain that we are going to have a "GLOWacracy" and elect a President of Camp GLOW. Explain the Presidential duties (described under number eight below).

5. Have a counselor deliver a dynamic mock election speech as an example of what the groups will be doing. Explain the steps of forming platforms and creating speeches.

6. Divide the group into campaign groups and have each group form a platform and write a speech. One person from each group should be elected to run for Camp GLOW President, along with a Vice President.

7. Give the groups plenty of time and materials to create campaign posters and props. Meanwhile, print up formal ballots and make a special ballot box to use for the elections.

8. Hold elections and have a party afterward to celebrate. The new president and vice president will have the duties of contacting other Camp GLOW presidents to share ideas; help start other Camps GLOW; give presentations in schools and in the community; and form a GLOW network/newsletter.

Learning how to rely on others   Lesotho

Part II – Congressional Session

The congressional session follows the election of the Camp GLOW president on the next day or night. The President leads the session, and the other campers sit in two half circles grouped by their region. In this session, goals are set for future Camp GLOW activities.

1. Discuss ideas presented in the election speeches (which may include Clubs GLOW, future camps, and ideas for keeping in touch).

2. Give the President a list to use when leading the discussion. She should choose an idea (one-by-one), state the idea to the congress, and then everybody has an opportunity to say why it was a good idea.

3. Have the Congress vote on whether or not an idea merits further discussion. If the Congress votes that "yes" the idea is a good idea, then they talk more about it, debate and decide how they can make the idea a reality.

Goal Setting and Achieving Lesson

Purpose: Learn what a goal is and to set up objectives as a way to plan for a successful future.

Desired Outcome: Campers will be able to set realistic goals and objectives in everyday life.

Part I – Explanation

1. Explain what a "goal" is using the analogy of a soccer team. Have one girl draw out a soccer field, and have her explain what happens during a soccer game.

2. Tell the campers that you have front row seats for everyone in the room to see Brazil play against (your country) in the Olympics. When you arrive in the arena where the games are being held, you notice that there is something strange about the field. The players are kicking the ball around, but nothing is happening. There are no goals. Explain that without goals, the game does not have a purpose. Same in life: if you have no goals, you are just on the field aimlessly kicking the ball around.

3. To develop goals, use this simple outline:

- Mission Statement: A brief sentence explaining what you want to accomplish
- WHAT: Be specific, explain the mission statement more here.
- WHO: the people who will help you toward your goals (explain the concept of networking)
- WHERE: a place, anywhere in the world
- WHEN: set up a timeline and a specific date
- HOW: Make lists of ideas to achieve goal (explain "to do" lists)
- WHY: Should refer back to the mission statement

For example:

Mission Statement: To go to university to study medicine

WHAT: To study to be a doctor

WHO: Parents, teachers, contacts from Camp GLOW, medical schools

WHERE: Local and national universities

WHEN: Study to take tests next year, to be in medical school within three years

HOW: Research what universities have medical courses of study; talk with doctor back home; contact friends and guest speakers from Camp GLOW; look in the newspaper and on the internet for information and, possibly, groups to support me emotionally or financially.

WHY: Because I have a lot to offer my community as a doctor

Part II – Phases of Goal Setting

1. Explain that when setting a goal you will miss a few shots. Famous Romanian soccer player, Hagi, did not walk off the field when he missed a shot. He is not considered a failure. Expect to have failures and challenges as you work towards your goals. Use a local athlete in your example.

2. The Four Phases (Draw a circle on the board and divide into 4 quarters; start with the upper right quarter and go clockwise.)

   • Phase 1 – The Honeymoon. The period when everything is perfect. Life is beautiful.

   • Phase 2 – Problems Arise. The period when everything fails. In this dark time, people tend to quit, give up. Seems like no answer in sight.

   • Phase 3 – Solutions to Problems. When you are determined to follow your goal, know that to each problem there is a solution. Be creative and open to new ideas.

   • Phase 4 – Growth. Once you have gone through this process, you have grown and you are excited and ready for more. The circle starts all over again.

3. Have the girls break up into small groups to write out their own goals. Take about seven minutes to have them loosely play with this outline (they can further explore this in the journal portion of the camp). Remind them that dreaming is FREE and does not cost a thing. Let them dream big, crazy and open to new things. Encourage their ideas and tell them that anything is possible if they really want to achieve it.

4. Have the small groups share. Use this model during other sessions such as decision-making or during the "Democracy Session" or "Community Service" session. See "Activities for Special Purposes" in Chapter Three in this ***Handbook***.

Resources: Kimberly Curry, PCV Romania, created this session for Junior Achievement workshops in Romania, which she lead throughout her Peace Corps service. Kimberly also gave this workshop during Camp GLOW.

"I Can't" Funeral

Purpose/Desired Outcome: Promote self-confidence and creative ways of thinking.

Do this activity in conjunction with a campfire. Have the campers think about things that they think they can't do. Then provide them with paper to write these things down. Have one counselor start by saying something like, "Yes, we are gathered here tonight to say goodbye to someone who has been around for a long time…". Then the counselor can move on to talk about the importance of believing in yourself, and not allowing others to tell you that you can't do something. Then, one by one, have the girls throw their "I can'ts" into the fire. Remember to bring pen and paper to the campfire for this activity.

Night Hike

Purpose: Promote group bonding and trust.

Desired Outcome: Hike will create a safe environment for sharing and learning.

No flashlights allowed! Begin around dusk. Have the girls link arms and walk with someone that they have not talked to before. Switch every five minutes or so.

Bring the girls to an open field. Play "Have you ever?" with them. A leader starts out in the center of a large circle with no open space (like in musical chairs). She asks a question, beginning with the words "Have you ever…" and ending with something she has done. It can be an embarrassing story, something silly, a favorite activity, or something ordinary. Whoever has done that thing must run to find a new spot on the circle. The leader looks for an opening and someone else is left standing in the center of the circle, who asks the next question, and so on. Play until it is dark. Everyone should join hands in the circle and the leader should begin the night trust hike.

During the daytime, investigate and select a patch of woods for the hike. When the leader encounters an obstacle, such as a ditch or log, she whispers it to the next girl and she passes the information down the line.

The hike should end in a clearing. Invite the girls to sit in a circle and light a candle. Begin a sharing time. Depending on the issues of the camp or within the group, it can be a directed sharing or an open one. The person who wishes to speak asks for the candle. Leaders should be prepared to begin the sharing process. This will allow the girls time to think of what they would like to share. When everyone has had a chance to share, extinguish the candle, and walk back to camp, hand in hand in a long line.

Shaking the Tree

Purpose/Desired Outcome: Self-empowerment and self-expression.

This activity was the theme of Camp GLOW in the Kyrgyz Republic, "shake up the tree of life to get more out of it." One Volunteer said, "Shaking the tree is about changing your life, changing traditions and empowering yourself." In a public space at your campsite hang a life-size tree made of paper with painted leaves. Encourage the campers to express their feelings and thoughts about traditions, empowerment, self-esteem, and other topics by writing on pieces of fruit cut from paper and pasting the fruit on the tree.

Sensory Awareness Trail

Purpose/Desired Outcome: Build trust within your group.

Set up a trail that campers walk through blindfolded, as they follow a rope. Set it up to have various objects hanging from the rope or objects that the rope crosses. With each object, participants must feel it, or smell it, or listen to it. Take precautions when setting this up to make sure that the pathway is clear of holes, rocks or anything that campers may trip over or bump into. Be creative!

SWOT

Purpose: Teach a skill for planning that can be used in many different scenarios.

Desire Outcome: Campers know how to use this skill and can apply it to their life and community.

Introduce the SWOT (strengths, weaknesses, opportunities, threats) analysis as a tool used by organizations, businesses, and social service agencies. The first two aspects assess the current state of the entity in discussion, while the second two aspects look towards the future. Together, practice creating one for the camp. Then, break up into groups and have the girls conduct a SWOT analysis for the community. Be sure to generate specific ideas, not generalities. If time remains, identify one need and create a plan to address it. For more information, see the "Goal Setting" and "Community Service" sessions in the "Activities for Special Purposes" section of Chapter Three.

Creative Expression

Collage

Purpose: Encourage self-expression and creative thinking.

Desired Outcome: Collage will serve as a means for the campers to think about their lives and futures.

Using markers, crayons, paper, stickers, magazines, objects from nature (grass, leaves, rocks) have campers make a collage representing themselves and their lives. To stimulate thought and ideas you can ask them to divide the collage into sections and answer certain questions such as: Where are you now? What are your goals? What are the principles by which you live?

Creative self-expression   Bulgaria

Doll-making

Purpose: Encourage self-expression and creative thinking.

Desired Outcome: Doll-making will serve as a means for campers to get in touch with the creative side of their personality.

Ask members of your community (fellow Volunteers and others) to donate scraps of materials, buttons, sequins, ribbon, yarn, thread, needles, and other things for doll making. Lead a session on creativity, the importance of self-expression and the idea of seeking your "inner child" or creative self. Throughout the week have the campers work on their dolls. Once the dolls are completed invite campers to share why each doll reflects them and what they learned from the experience.

Friendship Bracelets

Purpose: Encourage self-expression and have fun.

Desired Outcome: Girls will spend time together making bracelets and sharing about their lives.

Using embroidery floss, beads, or other local materials show students how to make bracelets. They are guaranteed to make creative variations on your original examples.

Journaling

Purpose: Promote self-expression, creative thinking and critical thinking.

Desired Outcome: Campers will develop a skill that they can use after camp ends. Counselors have found that journaling is a new activity for many campers and one that they take on with gusto and enthusiasm! Here are some ideas for leading an initial journaling session.

1. Draw a picture of a wrapped gift on a big piece of paper. Ask the girls what it might have to do with writing in your journal. Talk about how writing in your journal is like a gift to yourself for the future. Discuss how it helps you to remember your experiences, to see how you have changed, and to be able to look back.

2. Talk about why journaling is important to you. Discuss the confidentiality and privacy of someone's journal. Tell them if they want they can write in English during the camp, but that they do not have to.

3. Then, share the following ideas for getting started. Practice the first suggestion together. Be sure to ask the girls if they have any other ideas or suggestions.

Understanding the inner self   Russia

- Free writing: Write down your "stream of consciousness" [define for them], ignoring grammar and spelling, NON-STOP for 10 minutes. If you must begin with "I don't know what to write" over and over, do so until another idea appears. With this method, as you write, you empty out the "garbage" or miscellaneous thoughts on the surface until you get to the real, creative, powerful thoughts hidden beneath.

- Exercising: Write beginning with the phrases: I think, I feel and I want for 10 minutes each or take the first line of any poem or quote and complete it.

- Mix it up: Write sideways, upside-down, try writing without punctuation or capitalization or draw.

- Favorite place: Go to your favorite place to be alone. Write down only what you hear. Write down only what you see.

4. Stress that there is no right or wrong with journaling. Journals can be used for: drawing pictures, recording dreams, writing feelings, thoughts, ideas, doodling, writing addresses, recipes, writing stories, poems, writing reactions to books, films, things people say and do, recording goals and accomplishments.

Possible Journal Topics:

- Who is one woman that you admire, and why?

- How do you define leadership? What qualities are important?

- What do you hope to gain by participating in this leadership camp?

- What concerns do you have about the camp?

Self-confidence through journaling   Lithuania

Throughout the camp, encourage campers to use journals to record their thoughts and feelings about Camp GLOW. Consider scheduling time during the day or evening for the campers to journal.

Journal Decorating

Purpose: Encourage self-expression and creative thinking.

Desired Outcome: Girls will create a journal that reflects the personality of each camper.

Provide many materials for the girls to use such as stickers, markers, colored paper, magazines, stamps, and stamp pads. Suggest that the campers create a collage of pictures of things that represent them — who they are, what they like, things that are important to them, and dreams they have.

Music

Purpose/Desired Outcome: Encourage self-expression and creative thinking and to have fun.

Encourage campers who play an instrument to bring it along to camp. Create a camp songs sing-a-long sheet and schedule time for camp songs. Music and singing are great ways to energize a crowd and to bring the group together.

Poetry

Purpose: Encourage self-expression and creative thinking and have fun.

Desired Outcome: Show every camper that she has the ability to write poetry.

Teach the participants how to write various forms of poetry with (or without) a focus on nature.

- Haiku: has three lines of poetry, the first line of which contains five syllables, the second line contains seven, and the third line contains five syllables.

- Acrostic: The first letter in each line, when read vertically, spells out the name of something or conveys a message.

- Picture Poetry: forms a picture of what the poem is about.

- Free Verse: follows no set formula.

Environmental Activities

The Web of Life

Purpose/Desired Outcome: Demonstrate the interconnectedness of everything in the universe.

"When we try to pick out something by itself, we find it hitched to everything else in the universe." An ecosystem is like a piece of fabric; one thread pulled can unravel the whole complex weaving. Each component of the environment depends on another and perpetuates the web of life. Each component in the web of life has its own particular place and its own particular role to play. By altering one component of an ecosystem, there is an effect on all the others. This law of interconnectedness applies to all types of ecosystems in our environment. This activity provides a concrete example. In order to lead this activity you will need a ball of string and name cards displaying different elements of the environment.

1. Ahead of time write the elements cards (such as water, trees, birds) that will be in the web on separate pieces of paper in large print so that all can see them. Lay them out, and then ask each of the students to take one and tape it to their front or chair, that way everyone one in the circle can see what everyone else is.

2. Have the campers form a circle. Hand out the element cards and present the rationale behind this activity.

3. Start the game by looping the end of the ball of string around your finger. Explain that each person represents an element of the environment. Explain your card and its significant connection to its surroundings, i.e., another element card in the group. For example: I am a tree and I produce delicious fruit.

4. Throw the ball of string to the person in the circle who has the fruit card and have this person loop the string around a finger. This person thinks of another part of nature which links to the first statement. For example: I am the delicious fruit that is eaten by the bird.

5. This person then throws the ball to the person with the bird card who follows the same instructions. Continue until all group members have participated and the string intertwines into a web.

6. Point out that the web illustrates the complexity of relationships and interconnectedness found in nature.

7. Ask one of the campers to pull on the string and tell them that others who can feel this pull should raise their hand.

8. Next, ask one person to drop the string. Any others who are directly linked to that connection should also drop their strings. This chain reaction will continue until the web is destroyed.

9. Ask participants to explain the significance of this activity.

Environmental Commandments

Purpose: Further writing skills and self-expression.

Desired Outcome: Challenge participants to consider future activities.

Ask the campers to write "ten commandments" or personal goals to make positive changes in the world around them. Ask the campers to share some of their goals. This is a good closing activity for environmental camps.

Cleaning the environment can be fun   Bulgaria

Scavenger Hunt

Purpose/Desire Outcome: Make campers aware of their environment and have fun.

Create a list in the traditional scavenger hunt style, with a focus on the environment. Participants can work in pairs or in small groups. Set a time limit and give a prize to the winner.

Stargazing

Purpose: Have fun and demonstrate that we all can learn from one another.

Desired Outcome: Girls will have fun and develop a greater knowledge of the sky.

If someone in the group is knowledgeable about the night sky, have a stargazing night or go for a night hike and call for owls.

Environmental Fashion Show

Purpose/Desired Outcome: Have fun and think creatively.

Have campers create outfits using only things found in your environment.

Health Activities

Body Mapping

Purpose/Desired Outcome: Increase body image awareness.

Hand out large sheets of poster paper, one to each discussion group. On it should be drawn (ahead of time) an outline of a human form. Engage in a small discussion about how the way we feel about ourselves is a reflection of our feelings and attitudes toward the environment and vice versa. Ask each group to fill in the human outline with drawings of the body-environment connection. When the groups finish, they should present the body maps to the rest of the group with an explanation of their feelings.

Guest Speakers

Purpose/Desired Outcome: Share knowledge, resources, and provide role models.

Invite female doctors, community health workers, or other representatives to discuss questions and concerns that campers have about women's health issues. In the Philippines, counselors used the issues raised during the camp application process to prepare topics covered during the health sessions.

Nutrition

Purpose/Desired Outcome: Share knowledge and encourage healthy eating.

Many young women suffer from poor body image, which can lead to unhealthy eating habits and eating disorders. Reviewing the "food pyramid" or the different food groups can lead to a better understanding of what is required to fuel the body and maintain a healthy weight.

Relationships and Sexuality

Purpose/Desired Outcome: Address questions related to sex, sexuality, and relationships in an anonymous and safe environment.

Camp GLOW Romania called this session "Everything You Ever Wanted to Know about Sex and Relationships BUT Were Afraid to Ask."

Once you have clearly established trust in your group you may want to have a "sex and relationships" talk. Throughout the week at camp, have a "question box" in a central location and invite the campers to write any questions they have about sex, sexuality, and relationships and place them in the box. Question can be signed or anonymous.

Before the session, you may want to pass out information about AIDS, pregnancy, other women's health topics, or about sexual orientation. Tell the campers that they can come and talk to the counselors individually or write down any questions they have concerning this information. The "back–up" plan on the night of the talk can be to review the information in the brochures in case the discussion is not very lively.

During these talks, review the importance of confidentiality and then read the questions aloud. Next one or two of the counselors may talk briefly about the question (the counselors can read all of the questions before the session and plan who is going to say what). Then, you can open each question up and let anyone who wants to say anything share her ideas.

Stress and Relaxation

Purpose/Desired Outcome: Teach constructive ways to deal with stress.

Handling stress in a positive way is a skill for all of us to develop. Campers have really responded to activities and suggestions on how to cope with stress. Here are some suggestions to start that discussion with your campers.

- What is stress? (Elicit definition.)

  What causes stress? (e.g., school-work, parents, relationships)

  What are positive (e.g., sports, exercise, music, art) and negative (e.g., verbal abuse, physical abuse, nothing) ways to release stress.

- Meditation is a possible way to relax. What does meditation mean to you?

  a. Explain the breathing exercises, muscle-tension release exercises (see the "Yoga" section below), and visualization techniques. Play soft, gentle music in the background. For example, you may start a session by saying something such as:

Team building activity   Tanzania

You are in a place of total relaxation and peace, perhaps you are floating on a cloud in a clear blue sky; lying in a meadow surrounded by wildflowers; or sitting on the beach listening to the sound of the waves with the warm sun on your back. Take deep, gentle breaths and focus on the quiet of this lovely place, with each breath let go of the tensions of the day and feel the nurturing energy and peace that surrounds you.

Then give people a few moments to relax and breathe. After a few minutes, gently call people back to the present. Invite campers or counselors to share their experiences or give them time to journal.

b. Lead the group through yoga exercises (sun salutation) or stretching techniques as an introduction to other ways to relieve stress.

Yoga

Purpose: Teach a skill that can help deal with stress and encourage healthy lifestyle.

Desired Outcome: Campers will master this skill and use it in the future.

Counselors have introduced the concept of yoga during many Camps GLOW. It has been very popular as it is something concrete that the campers can practice at home. Here are some tips from Camp GLOW yoga experts.

Start with the most important thing in yoga, the "breath." It may sound easy, but it is the least practiced and most important exercise of Yoga.

1. Identify diaphragm: behind your belly button, your point of origin.

2. Get rooted: sit comfortably, legs crossed, shoulders and all muscles of the face, arms, stomach, and legs are relaxed. BACK IS STRAIGHT!!!

3. Inhale: begin at point of origin, fill belly with air, then chest, then throat. Hold for five counts.

4. Exhale: reverse the action, push down into belly, then use diaphragm to push belly button towards your lower back. Repeat.

*Always try to relax your tongue at its base.

Next exercise:

1. Lie on back, bringing legs to chest, hug knees and try to relax spine as much as possible. Relax neck muscles; slowly move head from side to side.

2. Bring head up to knees, then slowly lower both head and knees simultaneously. Lie flat.

3. Repeat, but alternating legs.

Next exercise: Neck roll

1. Simply roll neck slowly and gently starting right three times, then left.

2. Make sure shoulders are relaxed.

Physical Activities

All-Day Hike

Purpose: Team-building, accomplishing a goal, having fun.

Desired Outcome: Campers feel more confident in themselves.

A physically challenging hike can serve as a way to bring the group together. Along the trail, the group can stop for short environmental and sensory awareness activities. Make sure that at least two or three people know the trail well and can act as hike leaders. Develop a buddy system to check up on each other. Bring plenty of first aid kits, water, clothes for all kinds of weather, food, a couple of flashlights, pocketknife, etc., and of course, a good attitude. Be prepared for a couple of participants to stay behind with a counselor - assign a special task for them or take them on a shorter hike. Tell all the participants about the day hike before the camp starts so they can bring appropriate clothing and equipment.

GLOW Olympics

Purpose/Desired Outcome: Have fun and encourage team-building.

Have the girls in teams come up with a team name and a cheer. Emphasize the fun and de-emphasize the competition. Come up with a series of relay races and fun games such as a three-legged race and water-balloon toss.

Sports

Many sports activities such as swimming, kickboxing, aerobics, walking, jogging, baseball, soccer, jump rope, hopscotch, beach volleyball, and yoga (see the "Health" section above) have all been successful at different camps.

Working together towards a common goal   Lesotho

Special Camp Days and Nights

These are all fun "more traditional" camp activities that follow. Their purpose and goal is to help bring your group together and create fond memories.

Animal Masquerade and Ball

Make masks of your favorite animal and have a parade and then a disco with dance contests. (Hokey Pokey and Limbo!)

Birthdays

Celebrate any birthdays with a specially decorated chair for the honored person to sit in at meal times, a dessert at breakfast or a crazy hat that has to be worn all day. The more creative the birthday honor, the better.

Camp T-shirt Day

Have T-shirts made or make them yourself during camp with tie-dye. Have a camper design a camp logo and sew it on to all shirts or paint it on with spray paint, which is permanent. T-Shirt day is a good time for a group photo. In addition, camp T-shirts make great thank you gifts for those who have been an outstanding help in supporting your camp.

Discovering artistic talents   Russia

Cabin Cheer Contest/Cabin Identity

Whether your participants are in cabins or just rooms, this activity should work well and get spirits high. Tell your campers that you are going to have a Cabin Cheer contest. Give an example, something fun and silly such as:

> Camp GLOW Counselors
> It's no guess
> We're the coolest camp
> Here in Mures
> We're Anna, Laura Mike and Kim
> John, Amy, Linda, Sam and Jen
> Hey, everyone now listen close
> Here's a secret not to miss
> Listen, listen, listen (repeat getting softer)
> — PAUSE —
> (Yell) Camp GLOW ROCKS!!!

Next, pass out some supplies such as markers and paper. Give campers one hour to both decorate the door to their room and think of a cabin cheer that represents the qualities of their group. Have the counselor that is assigned to their room join in on the activity.

Afterwards have everyone perform their cheers and the counselors can "judge them." You can even decide on a tie — so everyone wins. This activity is tons of fun and gets the girls to know their cabin mates who are not from their towns.

Campfires

If you are fortunate enough to have a place at your camp where you can gather firewood and have a campfire, it can be both fun and a great bonding activity. If there is one or more camper who can play the guitar, you should encourage them to bring it to camp (find this out at your information sessions before camp). If there is a counselor who can play the guitar or who can lead singing without a guitar prepare a song-sheet and you are ready to go!

Movie Night

If a VCR is available, rent a film and serve popcorn and refreshments. This could serve as a good rainy day backup activity.

Talent Show

Let your talent GLOW! The last night of camp is a great time to have a talent show. Hopefully your campers will feel comfortable expressing themselves. It is also a chance to start the closure process, which can continue the next morning.

Part Four: Closing Activities

Sharing Bell

Purpose: Create a safe environment where each person has a chance to be heard and supported.

Desired Outcome: Campers will have a chance to share memories and create closure.

On the last day of camp, have campers and counselors sit in a circle. Pass around a small bell or some other object. The participant who has the bell may share something that they are feeling or something that they learned from camp. Campers are not required to talk if they do not want to, they may simply pause and hold the bell for a moment. If you do not have the bell, you should listen quietly. Have a counselor start and end the sharing circle. Have some tissues on-hand.

Human Chair

Purpose: Promote teamwork and have fun.

Desired Outcome: Participants will see how when people work together they can accomplish their goals.

Have everyone stand in a circle heel to heel. In order for this to be a success, everyone's feet need to be lined up perfectly. Then on the count of three, everyone sit down and if your feet are lined up right the circle should support itself.

Certificates

Purpose: Recognize and honor each camper.

Desired Outcome: Campers are proud of what they have accomplished and have something tangible to show for completing Camp GLOW.

Awarding accomplishments   Gabon

Make a certificate for each girl, signed by all the counselors, and hold a short graduation ceremony the last day of camp. See Appendix J for examples.

Nicknames

Purpose/Desired Outcome: Participate in a fun activity and recognize each camper for her individual strengths.

In the counselors' room or supply room, keep a list of the camper's names. Throughout the week, write down a funny, creative, interesting, thoughtful thing that they did or said. On the last day of camp, give out certificates to the campers with their new nicknames. Explain how they earned the name. For example, do you have a camper who loves to help with the campfire? Call her "fire starter" and tell her why. Do you have a camper who swam for the first time? Call her "super swimmer"!

CHAPTER 4: APPLICATIONS OF CAMP GLOW

In this chapter you will find information on Camps GLOW that have focused on specific areas including: environment, health, teaching English as a foreign language, involving boys and men in Camp GLOW, cultural understanding ,and democracy. Some Camps GLOW have had diverse foci depending on the community needs, skills of counselors, and interests of the participants. This section explores some of the ways Camp GLOW has offered leadership training while providing for the enrichment of campers in other areas.

ENVIRONMENT

Environmental awareness activities are present at many camps. Camps GLOW have also taken place where the primary goal was teaching about leadership and being stewards of the earth.

In the Philippines, the focus of Camp GLOW was to explore the connection between women and nature. Camp activities included teaching sessions on composting, biodiversity, and mountain, forest and marine ecology. Camp participants considered the theory of "eco-feminism"[3] within an appropriate cultural context. The report states that their "camp was a tool for the actualization of present and future dreams to be shared in a safe, positive, supportive environment which advocated living our lives in balanced relations with the earth and each other." Many guest speakers stressed the importance of women respecting and being the caretakers of the earth through their use of natural medicines, agricultural diversity, and making the world safe for their children. For examples of environmental activities, please see the "Activities for Special Purposes" section in Chapter Three of this *Handbook*.

In addition, other Camps GLOW have included environmental components. In Bulgaria campers did a "trash-pickup." On-going environmental activities may include involving GLOW clubs in an Earth Day celebration, community garden, composting, or recycling efforts.

---

[3] " The term 'ecofeminism' was coined by French writer Francoise d' Eaubonne in 1974 when she called upon the women to lead an ecological revolution to save the planet." Caroline Merchant, "Perspectives on Ecofeminism," *Environmental Action*, Summer 92, Vol. 24, Issue 2, p. 18.

HEALTH

A woman's knowledge of her body is an important step to her empowerment. Camp GLOW provides the space to answer questions and dispel myths about the female body and women's health issues. During past camps, counselors have invited local female doctors; translated educational materials into local languages; and held fora for campers to educate themselves about their health and issues related to women such as domestic violence and sexual harassment. For ideas on how to incorporate health activities into your camp see Chapter Three.

In Madagascar, on the island of Ste. Marie, Volunteers created a girls' camp to respond to the health needs of the local population. The principal issue facing young girls on Ste. Marie is that an increasingly large number turn to prostitution. This is a by-product of the tourist trade on that island and contributes to the high rate of HIV infection. The goal of the camp was to help girls make informed and responsible decisions. The objectives of the camp were to teach and discuss the truths of STDs and HIV/AIDs including the transmission and prevention of these illnesses. Other topics included self-esteem, career options, and presentations by Malagasy female role models. To ensure the sustainability of the project, Volunteers trained local high school girls to be the facilitators and presenters of the workshop. By encouraging peer education, the Volunteers set the stage for future camps.

TEACHING ENGLISH AS A FOREIGN LANGUAGE (TEFL)

English is the primary teaching language at many Camps GLOW. Therefore, all sessions are in English and applicants must demonstrate a proficiency in English in order to participate. Many students in Peace Corps countries study English but lack enrichment activities to improve their skills. Camp GLOW is an opportunity for students to use English outside of the classroom in a real life situation.

Volunteers have found that holding multi-ethnic camps (where campers are from different ethnic backgrounds) in English is a great way to have campers focus on their common future as women, instead of their different ethnicities.

Running Camp GLOW in English, however, can limit the number of local participants (particularly adults). Therefore, it is worthwhile to consider translating some camp materials if there is interest in holding follow-up GLOW activities in a local area.

At Peace Corps posts in places such as Africa or Latin America, conducting Camp GLOW in colonial languages such as French, Spanish, and Portuguese can have the same unifying effect as conducting a camp in English. Campers have a tool to bring them together through a common language and can focus on their similarities rather than their differences. In addition, more resources may be available such as printed materials in a colonial or official language.

> *[Because the camp was in English]… This was also a chance for Russian and Latvian speaking girls to come together in a non-threatening atmosphere where the focus was not on their various languages but on their future.*
>
> **Excerpt from the fiscal year 2000 English Education Project Status Report, Peace Corps/Latvia**

The *Camp GLOW Poland Manual 1999* suggests that future GLOW counselors distribute a vocabulary list with native language translation and explanations (there may be no direct translation) for words and concepts often used in Camp GLOW presentations. Some example words are:

ability	equal rights	respect	entrepreneur
achievement	freedom	responsibility	proud
assertive	friendship	schedule	to prepare
barrier	goal	self-esteem	Do It Yourself
body image	goal setting	self-respect	prejudice
budget	independent	skill	to limit
business	leader	sustainability	against women
capital	leadership	time management	power
capitalism	limitation	to accomplish	to change
discrimination	nature	to care	

INVOLVING BOYS AND MEN IN CAMP GLOW

In order to succeed in empowering women to be leaders, efforts to transform society must also incorporate men and boys. There have been several ways that Camps GLOW have included men and boys in these efforts.

One way is by having male counselors. According to camp evaluations, having men present at Camp GLOW shows the campers positive male role models who believe in women's leadership and skills. Campers come to a greater understanding that both men and women need to be open-minded and respect one another. Watching counselors of both sexes work together as equals gives campers a new model of leadership in action.

Developing common goals   Namibia

Another way boys can be involved in Camp GLOW is by creating separate boys camps that identify gender stereotypes and create a new model for thinking about gender issues and roles in society. Volunteers are developing new approaches to boys' leadership in places like Kazakhstan, the Kyrgyz Republic, Namibia, and Nicaragua.

The third way Camp GLOW can involve men and boys in girls' leadership is to hold parallel camps with a few mixed sessions as appropriate. In Namibia, a Camp GGLOW — Girls and Guys Leading Our World is being organized. In addition, boys are invited to attend certain club GLOW activities as appropriate, but the leadership of the clubs and the weeklong camp remain female.

Trust and teamwork   Namibia

It is important to note that the desire to include boys needs to come from the female campers themselves. In the case of Poland the boys' participation is defined by the female campers and conducted in a way that enhances the experience of the female campers.

Please see Chapter Two for further information on leadership materials relevant to boys.

CULTURAL UNDERSTANDING

Tensions between ethnic or socio-economic groups are realities and challenges to overcome when organizing Camp GLOW. Camps that incorporate girls from different backgrounds, can lead to campers' greater understanding and respect for others, which in turn makes better leaders.

In Latvia and Romania, counselors have successfully led Camps GLOW with campers from various ethnic groups. A key element to their success was using English as the language of the camp. Campers did not focus on what language people were speaking and instead could focus on content. During Camp GLOW in Romania, counselors placed campers in ethnically mixed dorm rooms with a native English speaker in each room. This helped to remove tension over language; campers spoke English consistently and got to know one another on an individual basis.

CHAPTER 5:
AT THE END OF CAMP

In this chapter, you will find information on steps to take to celebrate, evaluate, and report to all the individuals that have supported your camp.

CELEBRATION

As you reach the end of Camp GLOW be sure to celebrate your successes! Hold some kind of closing ceremony or graduation. Give campers and counselors a chance to share their experiences. Acknowledge both those people who are present and those who are not who made the camp possible. Enjoy your final moments together before you go back out into your different communities!

Enjoying final moments together   Russia

EVALUATION

A camp evaluation is an important element in concluding Camp GLOW, as it gives the campers a sense of closure; honors campers input; and is a good way for counselors to get concrete suggestions for improvement and feedback on what was successful.

- Create an evaluation form, asking specific questions about the workshops such as understanding and interest in topics presented and language comprehension. Also ask more general questions such as: likes and dislikes, suggestions, and if the campers might like to return to help with another Camp GLOW in the future. (See Appendix K for evaluation forms and Appendix L for a compilation of camp evaluations.)

- On the last day or night of camp, include some kind of activity to allow the campers to evaluate themselves. Have them write in their journals reflecting on what they feel and have learned. Encourage them to look back in their journals and read about their first night at camp. Where were they on their personal journeys BEFORE Camp GLOW and where do they feel they are now, AFTER completing Camp GLOW? Create a safe environment and opportunity for them to share. See the "Activities for Implementation" section in Chapter Three of this *Handbook* for more ideas on closing activities.

- Create an address list and send it out so that the participants can keep in touch with one another. When you mail out the address list, include a Camp GLOW group photo.

- It is also important for counselors and junior counselors to evaluate the camp. After the camp plan a time to discuss:

    - Camp GLOW evaluations from campers (ask someone to tabulate them).

    - What the counselors and junior counselors thought of the camp.

    - Lessons learned and a list of resources. Distribute this to Peace Corps Program Managers/ APCDs and the WID/GAD Coordinator in Washington. (This will help Volunteers, junior counselors and host-country nationals plan future Camps GLOW.)

REPORTING

When you finish your Camp GLOW, the hope is that you feel it was a worthwhile experience. After any momentous event, there are some wrap-up activities. One of these is writing reports. Sharing your knowledge and insights into Camp GLOW is a great way to "publicize" the camp and help ensure that it will continue in your host country and in your community. What you have learned through the Camp GLOW process is valuable and will be appreciated by community members and future Volunteers.

Reports to Donors

Donors should always receive a thank you letter in writing. In addition, many donors require some form of a grant report. In your grant report, include a summary of activities, touching or entertaining vignettes, a quote from a camper or counselor, or an excerpt from a camp evaluation form. In addition, include a breakdown of expenses or how you used certain supplies. Nice touches with a report may include: sending a photo or photos and a handwritten note from a camper to the donor. (See Appendix H for a grant report; see Appendix M for thank you notes.)

Reports for Peace Corps and Future Camps

Let your Program Manager/APCD know about your Camp GLOW. Include any information from the "Reports to Donors" (see above). In addition, incorporate any lessons learned, suggestions for a better camp, country specific camp information, lesson plans, and a host-country national contact list. This may be useful to future Volunteers or other Camp GLOW organizers.

Create a List of Potential Junior Counselors

If you have a few campers who you think would do well in a leadership role at a future camp, create a list of their names and addresses and include them in your camp materials.

Give Presentations

Offer to speak to other Peace Corps Volunteers about Camp GLOW at In-Service Trainings or Pre-Service Trainings. Look for opportunities in your community to talk about Camp GLOW and its benefits.

If possible, besides giving your Program Manager/APCD a copy of your Camp GLOW Report or Camp GLOW Manual, place a copy of it in your Peace Corps Resource Room. Also, pass out your report to all host-country nationals who participated in your camp. Consider having some materials translated into the local language.

Peace Corps/Washington would enjoy receiving a copy of your camp materials. Please send your Camp GLOW report to:

Women in Development/Gender and Development Coordinator
Peace Corps/The Center
Paul D. Coverdell Peace Corps Headquarters
1111 20th Street, NW
Washington, DC 20526
USA

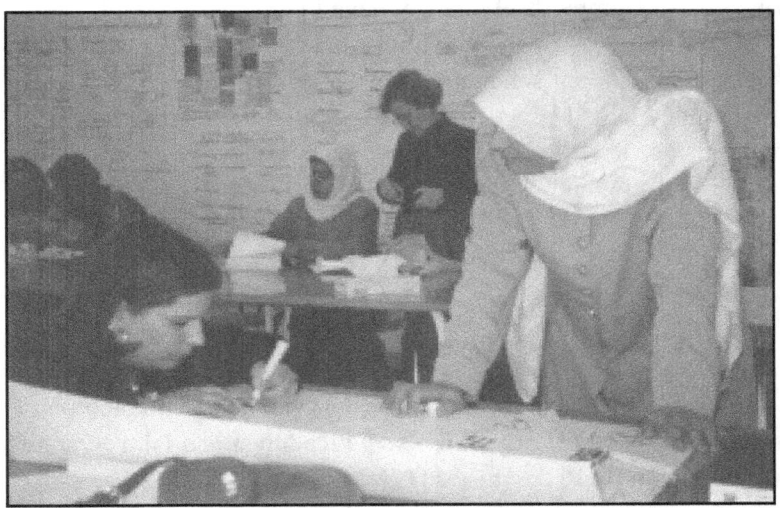

Goal setting   Jordan

CHAPTER 6: TAKING THE EXPERIENCE HOME

In this chapter, you will find concrete ideas to help the spirit of Camp GLOW continue once campers return home. Topics covered in this chapter include: GLOW Clubs; ways to keep in touch, follow-up with teachers, parents, and other community members; and a brief conclusion to this *Handbook*.

ON-GOING ACTIVITIES WITH STUDENTS WHO PARTICIPATED IN CAMP GLOW

During Camp GLOW a close-knit community forms. Returning home after camp can sometimes be challenging to campers (and counselors). Once the campers return to their homes and schools, they often want to gather with others who have experienced Camp GLOW to discuss how what they have learned applies to everyday life. Following Camp GLOW, many campers are enthusiastic and full of great ideas of how to make a difference in their communities. Supporting campers in small groups and helping them to channel their energy are great ways to reinforce and expand their leadership skills.

The spirit and principles of Camp GLOW do not have to end at the end of camp. Many innovative campers have gone on after camp to teach in their schools (to boys and girls alike) about what they have learned and how to use these skills every day. This chapter discusses some ideas for community outreach and on-going activities with GLOW campers.

> *Camp GLOW focuses on the preparation of oneself for leadership, but the practice of 'leadership-in-action' is essential to solidifying what was learned at camp.*
>
> **Camp GLOW Counselor**

GLOW CLUBS

In many ways, on-going work with campers is the best way to help them incorporate what they have learned into their lives. Around the world, campers with adult support are creating GLOW Clubs in their schools and communities. In Romania, GLOW Clubs meet monthly. The goal of these clubs is to continue to encourage the girls to develop themselves as leaders by discussing relevant topics, supporting each other, and practicing leadership skills through community service projects. Girls have been visiting orphanages and educating their peers at school in what they learned at camp. They have also taught classes in English on self-esteem, conflict resolution, decision-making and setting goals.

In Poland, GLOW Clubs have developed into a network. They organize regional camps during the school year and larger national camps during the summer. Students are actively involved in fundraising by holding events such as discos, car washes, bake sales, and selling hand-made cards.

Here are some suggested activities from adults engaged in on-going projects with GLOW Clubs. See Appendix N for an information sheet from Poland to help campers get started on forming a club.

- Conduct group SWOT (Strengths, Weaknesses, Opportunities, Threats) analysis with your Club GLOW, the community-at-large or one section of a community to brainstorm community needs. Discuss how young people can be community leaders and give examples of young women and men who have made a difference. See Chapter Three for more information on SWOT.

- Get specific about community service — brainstorm a list of issues that are important to the community. Have the girls identify issues with which they can become involved and give ideas on how they can make an impact. Have them form committees based on what they would most like to work with. Each committee should have an adult helper to assist the girls as needed. Each committee should plan a service project. Some examples of community service projects include: peer education in GLOW Camp topics; visiting children in orphanages or hospitals; visiting the elderly; educating younger students in GLOW Camp topics; community education in topics such as sexual education, AIDS, abuse of alcohol,

Coping with stress   Bulgaria

tobacco, and other drugs; sexual harassment and domestic violence; work with street children and the homeless; or work on habitat and shelters. For a sample lesson plan, see Chapter Three.

- Provide information on issues identified as important to the community and examples of ways that people are working on them around the world.

- Highlight leadership activities by inviting girls to share what they have been involved in through interviews and presentations. Girls will inspire one another in this way.

- Conduct training on project planning and proposal writing. This could be a very important skill for girls to have and could help them find a local sponsor if their service project needs funding.

- Invite inspiring local women leaders to come and speak frankly with the girls about their lives and choices. Be sure to save time for the girls to ask questions. This can be a very important way for GLOW girls to realize that not just foreigners are concerned about them and there are role models in the community. In a Romanian town, the only female politician of a local party came to speak to the girls at their GLOW club meeting. They had many questions about how she became a leader within the constraints of society. Her message "that young women are able to do anything that they want to" is one that the girls are not used to hearing. She was an important and inspiring example for them.

- Ask the group to write an accordion poem for expressing struggles and accomplishments anonymously. Give the starting lines and have each girl add one line, not looking at the previous ones, such as: "Looking back over the passing of time, we see challenges faced…. Yet we focus on experiences of growth in our lives…." When completed, read the poem aloud.

- Have girls collect items from the ground — sticks, stones, leaves, bits of trash, flowers — and have them "recreate the GLOW camp" working in groups. Then have each group cooperatively explain what they created. Counselors leading this activity after camp found that the girls came up with literal and figurative models that recalled experiences that had touched them – some funny, some profound. They also recalled the camp atmosphere and what they learned at camp through this activity.

- Share within the group something about camp: one thing you learned at GLOW Camp, one positive thing you have done as a result of the camp, most fun activity, most important topic, most personally meaningful moment.

- Discuss women's leadership: characteristics of a woman leader, challenges faced by women leaders, role models of women leaders.

- Hold "get to know yourself" activities and skill building activities, such as conflict resolution, personality or value inventories and developing communication skills.

- Hold sharing circles — pass around an object and let each girl have time to share goals, hopes, aspirations, expectations, experiences or inspirations.

- Focus on important women in our world by having the girls nominate and vote for the Annual GLOW Women Awards. Utilize categories such as athlete, singer, writer, actress, politician, local community leader, female character and an important women's issue.

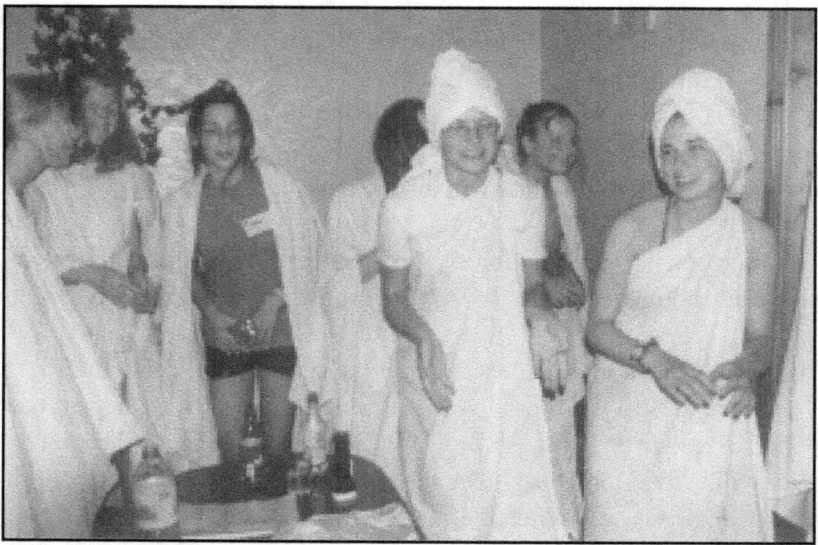

Celebrating traditions   Lithuania

- Create a Camp GLOW publication. In Poland, former campers have started a magazine called "Iron Daisies" that provides girls with a forum to share stories, ideas and poems that are important to them. The organizational process of publishing a magazine is great skill development exercise for the girls as well as a great leadership opportunity.

- Set up a pen pal system, a newsletter or arrange a GLOW reunion if the campers that attended Camp GLOW are from different towns.

- Create Camp GLOW materials that are easy and useful resources for clubs. Consider translating them into the local language or creating a GLOW club manual with some lesson plans from camp.

FOLLOW-UP WITH TEACHERS, PARENTS AND OTHER COMMUNITY MEMBERS

Camp GLOW and the activities that follow the camp are probably going to pique the interest and curiosity of parents, teachers, and friends close to a camper. Parents can bolster your community support and including them can provide benefits to the whole family. Exposing teachers to interactive teaching methods (like those at Camp GLOW) is a great way to transfer skills. Here are some ideas for including parents, teachers, and friends.

- Highlight leadership activities by inviting girls to share what they have been involved in through interviews and presentations. Have a family night where girls show photos and explain what they learned at camp.

- Have the girls present or lead an activity such as goal setting. Before the workshop, have the girls brainstorm how their goal setting model can be adapted for use within a family. For a sample lesson plan, see the "Activities for Special Purposes" section in Chapter Three of this *Handbook*.

- Arrange a family group activity. Have each family make a "family shield" or collage that represents different things such as one unique quality of each family member, a favorite family saying, a favorite memory, etc.

Transfering skills   Bulgaria

- Arrange a "GLOW Olympics" with siblings and friends invited to attend. Afterwards serve refreshments. This can also be a fundraiser for on-going GLOW projects.

- Hold an interactive training workshop for teachers on the Camp GLOW curricula. Stress both the content of Camp GLOW and interactive teaching methods. During the workshop, ask participants to give mini-presentations to reinforce what they have learned.

- Arrange for a conference to teach Volunteers and Counterparts about Camp GLOW if they have not participated in the camp before.

- Develop lesson plans based on Camp GLOW topics such as goal setting and decision-making. Hold trainings on these topics for the TEFL teachers in your schools.

Recognizing leaders   Lesotho

JUNIOR COUNSELORS

Using Junior Counselors is another way to keep former campers involved in Camp GLOW. Please see the "Selecting Campers, Junior Counselors and Counselors" section in Chapter Two of this *Handbook* for more information.

EMAIL DISCUSSION GROUP

An Email list serve is a way that counselors and campers can stay in touch and share experiences about Camp GLOW. Volunteers have created list serves in the past to share ideas about fundraising, recruitment and successful activities. If you want more information about WID/GAD list serves or girls' leadership list serves, contact the Peace Corps WID/GAD Coordinator at the address listed on page 61.

WRAP-UP/ CONCLUSION

Camp GLOW has a positive impact on and changes the lives of both campers and counselors. We hope that you find the materials in this *Handbook* useful as you plan your camp. We wish you the best of luck and encourage you to have fun whether this is your first Camp GLOW or your tenth! Remember that the possibilities for Camp GLOW are endless and the potential lies with those who participate in it. Be creative and innovative! By choosing to work with young women through Camp GLOW, you will undoubtedly plant many seeds of hope, leadership and encouragement. We hope that you gain as much as you give as you organize and facilitate your camp!

Chorus of the Camp GLOW song, written by Romanian campers:

Camp GLOW is our song,
We're happy to sing it,
We're all so proud,
We're coming round,
The bonds we've shared,
Will last forever,
We'll always be,
The same great friends,
The same great friends.

CAMP GLOW MOROCCO LINE ITEMS

Itemized Budget

Line Item	Amount
Total funds received	
Total amount earmarked for conference center	
Food	
Lodging	
Bedding	
Meeting rooms	
Total amount dispersed by village/region	
Total Expenditures to date from this amount	
Remaining funds being used for manuals	
Expenditures:	
Supplies	
Camper manual production	
Typing/printing	
Photocopies	
Photo developing	
Banner materials	
Banner painting	
Snacks	
Translations	
Travel Expenditures:	
PCV and accompanying camper and counterpart transport	
Camper and trainer transport to campsite	

APPENDIX B

Included in this appendix are three schedules to show the variety of topics covered during different camps. When creating your master schedule you should note who is responsible for leading/facilitating each activity and what materials the facilitator will need. It is not included here for space reasons.
• Camp GLOW Armenia's schedule includes many special guest speakers and a focus on career development.
• Camp GLOW Poland's schedule reflects a traditional Camp GLOW curriculum.
• **Camp GLOW Romania's schedule emphasizes social issues facing Romanian women and healthy relationships.**

CAMP GLOW ARMENIA SCHEDULE OF ACTIVITIES

Time	Sunday	Monday	Tuesday	Wednesday	Thursday	Friday	Saturday
8:30 – 9:15		Breakfast/Meeting with jr. counselors	Breakfast/Meeting with jr. counselors	Breakfast/Meeting with jr. counselors	Breakfast/Meeting with jr. counselors	Breakfast/Meeting with jr. counselors	Breakfast Meeting with jr. counselors
9:15 – 9:45		Daily introduction/ exercise	Daily introduction/ exercise	Daily introduction/ exercise	Daily introduction/ exercise	Daily introduction/ exercise	Daily introduction/ exercise
10:00 – 11:15		Special speaker: Personality	Special speaker: Personality	Special speaker: Women & Relationships	Special speaker: Career	Recap of the past week events	Camp 2001 leaders meeting
11:30 – 12:45		Special speaker: Health	Special speaker: Health	Special speaker: Women & Relationships	Special speaker: Career Development	Teamwork activity	Write personal statements
13:00 – 14:00		Lunch	Lunch	Lunch & pack snacks	Lunch	Career fair & finger foods	Leave for home
14:00 – 15:15	All campers meet in Yerevan (south camp)	Special speaker	Special speaker	Guided excursion to Hagerstein	Special speaker: Career Development		
15:30 – 16:45		Art activity (journal)	Special speaker	....	Art activity (t-shirts)		
17:00 – 18:00	Pot luck dinner	Computer lessons (optional)	Computer lessons (optional)	Computer lessons (optional)	Computer lessons (optional)		
18:00 – 19:00		Dinner	Mexican dinner		Italian dinner	Candle lighting ceremony	
19:00 - ?	Introduction/ Ice breaker	GLOW Olympiad	Movie night	Bonfire/dinner	Pamper yourself activity	Talent show/disco	
23:00	Sleep time!	Lights out!	Good night!	Sleep tight!	Don't let the bed bugs bite!	Have fun!!!!	

CAMP GLOW POLAND SCHEDULE OF ACTIVITIES

Time	June 30	July 1	July 2	July 3	July 4	July 5	July 6	July 7
7:30-8:15		Aerobics	Aerobics	Aerobics	Aerobics	Aerobics	Aerobics	
8:30-9:15		Breakfast	Breakfast	Breakfast	Breakfast	Breakfast	Breakfast	8am Breakfast
9:15-11:00		Team-building/ Doll-making	Hiking	Stress and relaxation/ Decision-making	Guest Speakers - LA Strada/ KARAT	Goal setting/ Skills and careers	Tolerance & Diversity/ Scavenger hunt	Evaluations 10:30 Departure
11:00-11:15		Break	Hiking	Break	Break	Break	Break	
11:15-13:00		Doll-making/ Team-building	Hiking	Decision-making/ Stress and Relaxation	Democracy/ Kickboxing and self-defense	Aggressive, assertive/Skills and careers	Tolerance & Diversity/ Scavenger hunt	
13:00-14:00	Chartered bus	Lunch	Lunch	Lunch	Lunch	Lunch	Lunch	
14:00-15:45	Arrival and Check-in	Self-esteem/ Attitudes	Values/ Human Rights	Expressing ourselves/ Self-portraits	Kickboxing/ Democracy	Goal setting/ Aggressive, assertive	Healthy Lifestyles Lifestyles with Carol	
15:45-16:00	Break	Break	Break	Break	Break	Break	Break	
16:00-17:45	Welcome and Intro (Icebreakers)	Self esteem/ Attitudes	Values/ Human Rights	Self portraits/ Expressing ourselves	Resolutions CEE conf. 17:00 break sandwiches	CEE women's rights conference	Popeye – problem-solving with Bob	
17:45-18:30	Free	Free	Free	Free	Free	Free	Doll pres.	
18:30-19:30	Dinner	Dinner	Dinner	Dinner	19:30 Campfire	Dinner	Certificates, awards	
19:30-21:00	Journal Writing	Skits	Game night	T-shirt tie-dying	Campfire	Talent Show	Campfire	
21:00	Staff Meeting	Staff Meeting	Staff Meeting	Staff Meeting	Staff Meeting	Staff Meeting	Staff Meeting	

CAMP GLOW ROMANIA SCHEDULE OF ACTIVITIES

Time	Sunday	Monday	Tuesday	Wednesday	Thursday	Friday	Saturday
7:30– 8:30		Wake-up	Wake-up	Wake-up	Wake-up	Wake-up	Wake-up
8:30-9:30		Breakfast and Announcements	Breakfast and Announcements	Breakfast and Announcements	Breakfast and Announcements	Breakfast ands Announcements	Breakfast and Announcements
9:30– 11:30		Self-esteem & IALAC*	Gender Roles & Values	Conflict Resolution & Relationships	Decision-making & Assertiveness	Status of Women in Romania	Thank you notes, Evaluation, Sharing Circle
11:30-12:30		Journaling	Journaling	Journaling	Journaling	Journaling	Journaling
12:30-13:30		Lunch	Lunch	Lunch	Lunch	Lunch	Lunch
13:30-15:00		Rotation Activity A: Team-building	Rotation Activity A: Team-building	Rotation Activity A: Team-building	Rotation Activity A: Team-building	Rotation Activity A: Team-building	Pack up
15:00-16:30	Travel to Village/ Settle In	Rotation Activity B: Women's Health: Nutrition & Body Image	Rotation Activity B: Goal Setting	Rotation Activity B: Domestic Violence	Rotation Activity B: Responding to Sexual Harassment	Rotation Activity B: Community Needs Assessment – SWOT	Chores
16:30-18:00	Camp Icebreakers	Rotation Activity C: Journal Decorating	Rotation Activity C: Yoga	Rotation Activity C: Friendship Bracelets	Rotation Activity C: Scavenger Hunt	Rotation Activity C: Talent Show Prep	Travel Back Home
18:00-19:00	Camp Rule Setting	Free Time	Free Time	Free Time	Free Time	Free Time	
19:00-20:30	Dinner	Dinner & Chores	Dinner & Chores	Dinner & Chores	Dinner & Chores	Dinner & Chores	
20:30-22:30	Journaling/ Free Time	Silly Olympiad	Night Hike	Camp Fire-Singing & S'mores	Sexuality questions & answers	Talent Show & Party	
22:30-23:30	Bedtime	Bedtime	Bedtime	Bedtime	Bedtime	Bedtime	Bedtime

PACKING LIST FOR GIRLS LEADING OUR WORLD (GLOW) CAMP IN ROMANIA

Here is a list of suggestions of what you should bring to camp with you. None of the items listed below are required and some may not be relevant to you. All meals and your bedding (sheets and blankets) will be provided at the camp.

While packing, remember, the most important packing rule: if you bring it, you carry it! Try to keep your luggage light and be considerate of others; we will have limited space on the bus to bring everything to camp. You are limited to one bag per person.

See you at the camp!

Clothes

- Shoes, a pair of comfortable walking shoes for hiking and sports such as sneakers or hiking boots. (No high heel platform shoes!)
- T-shirts
- Bathing suit
- A sweater or sweatshirt (We will be in the mountains and it could be cool at night)
- Shorts and a pair of pants or jeans
- Socks and underwear (panties and bras)
- Pajamas or a nightgown to sleep in
- A pair of slippers or sandals to wear around the dormitory

Outdoor Gear

- Sunscreen
- An empty plastic bottle for water such as a soda-pop bottle
- Hat or sunglasses as protection from the sun
- Rain gear such as a coat and/or umbrella

Bathroom

- Towel
- Hygiene products such as toothbrush, toothpaste, soap, shampoo, hairbrush, feminine sanitary napkins/ tampons

Other

- Your favorite music cassettes with your name on them
- A musical instrument, if you play one and want to share your talents!
- A pair of scissors for art projects
- Your spirit of creativity and openness

CAMP GLOW –
GIRLS LEADING OUR WORLD!
CALL FOR APPLICANTS

Where:

When:

Who: Girls aged 13 – 17

What is Camp GLOW?

Camp GLOW is a camp dedicated to girls' leadership development. Girls aged 13-17 participate in group activities focusing on teamwork, self-esteem, goal setting, and career development. Camp GLOW offers an opportunity for these young women to openly discuss their opinions regarding themselves, the world, and the future of both together. In addition to these activities, the girls also participate in a variety of team games, sports, songs and campfire fun.

How Much English Do I Need?

Camp GLOW is conducted mainly in English, so a level of English proficiency is necessary. This does NOT mean that students must be fluent in the language or at the top of their class. ALL interested girls will be considered.

How Do I Apply?

All interested girls (ages 13-17) are asked to attend a short essay writing competition on (DATE) at (TIME) at (LOCATION). These essays will be read by a panel of Volunteers from around Romania and will be used to determine acceptance to the camp.

- The questions will NOT be handed out in advance.
- The total time to complete the essays will be 1 1/2 hours.
- Bring 2 pens and paper with you to the competition.
- Applicants will be notified of their acceptance to the camp by (DATE).

How Much Does It Cost?

NOTHING!!! This camp is FREE OF CHARGE to all participants. A deposit of AMOUNT will be needed to secure your place in the camp. The money WILL BE RETURNED TO YOU at the end of the camp. If this money is a problem, PLEASE STILL APPLY! Individual cases can be discussed after acceptance.

Any More Questions?

If you have any more questions, please contact _____.

ACCEPTANCE LETTER

Dear Applicant,

Congratulations! You have been accepted to Camp GLOW which will take place from DATE to DATE. We are very excited to have you as part of this camp and look forward to a great camp experience.

We will have a meeting on DAY and TIME. Let us meet inside the _____. It is very important (obligatory) that you attend this meeting. At this meeting, you will receive your health form, a packing list, and further details about the camp. It will also be a time for you to ask any questions you may have. Your parents and /or guardians are invited to attend this meeting if they have any questions.

When you come to the meeting, you need to bring the deposit of AMOUNT, which will be refunded at the end of the camp as long as you follow our three main rules: no smoking, drinking, or drugs. If you have any questions or concerns about the deposit, please let us know.

If you are unable to accept this invitation to Camp GLOW, please contact us immediately. There are other girls hoping to go to the camp and waiting for a place to open up.

Get ready for a GREAT camp experience!

Sincerely,

Camp GLOW Coordinators

WAIT-LIST LETTER

Dear Applicant,

Thank you for your application to Camp GLOW. We were impressed by your application. We had a large number of girls apply for the camp. Unfortunately, we are not able to accept all the girls that we would like to have at this camp. At this time, we would like to put your name on a waiting list for the camp. This means that if a place opens up in the camp you will be notified immediately of your acceptance. You will be notified by DATE, at the latest, if there will be a place for you at the camp.

Three people graded the application essays anonymously. Each of the five questions was graded on a scale of one to five. Though we emphasized the content of your ideas, an additional score was given for clarity of English. We were happy to have students from four local High Schools and three grade levels (9, 10, 11) participate in the essay contest, and the participants of the camp will reflect that balance.

Our hope is to have future GLOW Camps and various local activities. We encourage you to participate when the opportunity exists.

Thank you for your interest.

Sincerely,

Camp GLOW Coordinators

NON-ACCEPTANCE LETTER

Dear Applicant,

Thank you for applying to Camp GLOW. We were very impressed by your application. Unfortunately, due to a limited number of spots at the camp, we were unable to accept your application.

Three people graded the application essays anonymously. Each of the five questions was graded on a scale of one to five. Though we emphasized the content of your ideas, an additional score of one to five was given for your clarity of expression in English. We were happy to have students from four local High Schools and three grade levels (9, 10, 11) participate in the essay contest, and the participants of the camp will reflect that balance.

Our hope is to have future GLOW Camps and various local activities. We encourage you to participate when the opportunity exists.

Thank you for your interest.

Sincerely,

Camp GLOW Coordinators

APPENDIX F

CAMP GLOW 2000
PERMISSION SLIP AND
MEDICAL INFORMATION

Camp GLOW will take place from DATES. The camp will include young women from local high schools and will be facilitated by local women and Peace Corps Volunteers from the United States. Participants will be involved in English-language discussions and activities, focusing on topics like self-esteem, relationships, decision-making, and leadership. Outdoor activities, campfires, a talent show, and artistic activities will also be important parts of the camp.

All participants have agreed not to smoke, drink alcohol, or use illegal drugs, during the camp. Any participants who smoke, drink, or use drugs, will be sent home. We have asked participants to secure their place by making a deposit of AMOUNT. This deposit will be refunded at the end of the camp, as long as the participant has followed the above agreement.

Participants Name: _____

Parent's/Guardian's Name: _____

Relationship to Camp Participant: _____

Address: _____

Phone Number: _____

Second Contact: _____

Relationship to Camp Participant: _____

Phone Number: _____

Please list any allergies the participant has:

Please list any medication the participant will be bringing to the camp:

I understand the nature of Camp GLOW 2000 and that my daughter will be attending.

_____
Guardian's Signature

Please note that this permission slip was translated into the local languages.

LETTER REQUESTING
THE NOMINATION OF CAMPERS
Sample from Bulgaria

Date

Dear Colleagues,

I am organizing a summer camp for teenage girls, ages 14 to 18 in TOWN. The camp is from DATES at LOCATION and will be free to participants. This project has several different aims: to increase self-esteem, teach leadership skills, improve English, and foster volunteerism. We will achieve these goals through small group discussions, games, sport activities, and community excursions. The curriculum has it basis in the Camp GLOW (Girls Leading Our World) that was highly successful in Romania and Poland. This will be the first GLOW camp in Bulgaria. By working with at least seven American Volunteers and Bulgarian High School Teachers, participants will gain new skills and have an extremely fun week.

I wish all English students could participate in this activity. However, there are a limited number of spaces available. In order to make it as fair as possible, I am asking for your help. I am asking English teachers from the NAME of SCHOOLS to select students from their classes. I can accept NUMBER girls from your school. Students should vary in ages from the __ to the __ class. I trust that you will make the best decisions on who will benefit the most from Camp GLOW.

You should evaluate your students based on the following criteria:
* Leadership skills – A student who demonstrates leadership abilities or who has the potential to be a good leader.
* Positive attitude – The student must be cooperative, have an open attitude towards new activities, and be motivated to think creatively.
* Good knowledge of English – It is not necessary that the student be the most advanced in the class, but that they should be able to understand and communicate in English with minimal difficulty.
* Availability – The student must be able to attend the summer camp from HOURS, DATES.

While the camp (supplies, staff, location) is free to participants, it will not provide transportation costs to and from the CAMP LOCATION or lunch. However, we will provide through our fundraising efforts, T-shirts, crafts, sports equipment, snacks and the costs of excursions.

Please select your students no later than DATE. Once you have chosen the students, please give them the enclosed information sheet/registration form (See Apendix E). I will notify each student about a pre-camp meeting where she will receive details about Camp GLOW. If you have any questions, concerns, or comments, PLEASE contact me: by phone _____ or Email _____. I appreciate your help tremendously and recognize that this would not be possible without your guidance.

Sincerely,

APPENDIX G

Sample from Poland

NAME and ADDRESS
NAME of INSTITUTION (if applicable)

Attention: English Teachers
RE: Camp GLOW (Girls Leading Our World)

Camp GLOW (Girls Leading Our World) is a leadership conference for young women, ages 13–19, to help prepare them for their emergence into adulthood. Camp GLOW will provide sessions for leadership skills, building self-esteem, career planning, and goal setting. It will be held DATES and LOCATION. The conference will consist of 35 girls (3 applicants from each major county) with their transportation, lodging and meals free of charge.

The conference requires speaking in the English language, therefore, all participants must have an average English grade of four or higher. We would like to request your help as the students' teachers and mentors in choosing the participants as the selection process is very difficult. We would prefer our students to be active in the classrooms, cooperative, team-oriented, and have a positive attitude.

If you have trouble choosing 3 students, please use one or both of the following questions as an essay question to assist you in your decision:

1. What kind of future do young women have in YOUR COUNTRY?

2. Is the future of YOUR COUNTRY'S young women changing? How?

The deadline for submitting the names of applicants is DATE.

Please feel free to contact Peace Corps Volunteer _____ with any further questions.

Contact information:

Thank you for your cooperation and we look forward to your submitted applications!

Sincerely,

Name
Peace Corps Volunteer

Camp GLOW will be run by American Peace Corps Volunteers serving throughout Poland . It is funded by the Democracy Commission Small Grants Program through the American Embassy.

PEACE CORPS PARTNERSHIP
QUARTERLY REPORT GUIDELINES

(To be sent to OPSC&IV every fiscal quarter – March, June, September, and December)

PCV Name:
Project name/number:
Quarterly Report # _____
Project Start Date:

Please use additional pages to fully describe the following:

1. Please give a detailed narrative report of the current status of your project.

2. What have been the major successes to date? What have been the biggest obstacles? How do you foresee overcoming those obstacles? How is your project contributing to building capacity within the community?

3. Give a detailed account of your expenditures to date:

Budget Line Item	Individual Expense	Cumulative Expenses
Totals		

4. Has your community participated as expected? Do you feel they have a sense of "ownership" of the project? Have the members helped in realizing the project goals and objectives on a daily basis? Have they demonstrated a systematic approach to planning, monitoring, and evaluation? Have they supplied the necessary money or in-kind donations for the project?

5. What indicators have been set up by you and your community to measure successes upon completion of your project?

6. Please provide a timeline to describe the next phase of your project/future plans.

7. Additional comments/suggestions.

PCV Signature_____ Date_____

PEACE CORPS PARTNERSHIP
FINAL REPORT GUIDELINES

(To be sent to OPSC&IV upon project completion)

PCV Name:
Project Name/Number:
Project Start Date:
Project Completion Date:

Please use additional pages to fully describe the following:

1. Please give a detailed narrative report of the current status of your project.

2. What were the major successes of this project? What were the biggest obstacles? How did you overcome those obstacles? Did the focus of the objectives change as the project progressed?

3. Give a detailed account of your expenditures to date:

Budget Line Item	Individual Expense	Cumulative Expenses
Totals		

4. Describe your community's reaction upon project completion. Do you think a transfer of knowledge/skills took place?

5. Share your conclusions or recommendations resulting from the experience of the project. Did you obtain your expected outcome (did the indicators you set up in your quarterly reports show the project results you hoped to achieve)? Would you do this type of project again?

6. Will there be recurring costs coming out of this activity? How does the community plan to cover these costs?

7. Additional comments/suggestions.

PCV Signature _____ Date _____

CAMP GLOW POLAND
GRANT PROPOSAL[1]

Name of the Institution:
ORGANIZATION NAME:
Address:
email:

Name and Title of Grant Writer/Project Director:

Information on the institution requesting the grant:
The NAME OF ORGANIZATION is a non-governmental organization (NGO) that originated as a committee which participated in the Fourth Annual UN World Conference on Women in Beijing, China, 1995. In the aftermath of the Conference, the Committee continued to promote the ideas generated in Beijing. In 1998, the ORGANIZATION was officially incorporated as an NGO. Its activities concentrate on the following issues: empowerment for women, human rights, equality among men and women in decision-making and within the economic, social, cultural, and political spheres, to name a few. It also monitors governmental and political activities (or the lack of them) concerning equal status for women. In addition, a major project of the Association is the KARAT Coalition, a network of women's NGOs in the Central and Eastern European (CEE) region.

Juridical status, date of registration:
Juridical status: See attachment
Date of Registration: DATE

Financial or in-kind contributions made in the past:
Not applicable

Project Description:
Camp GLOW (Girls Leading Our World) is a weeklong English language and leadership training camp for young women, aged 15–19, from southeastern Poland. The camp will be held in VILLAGE from DATES.

The camp's goals are as follows:
1) to develop leadership skills, including:
    a) public-speaking;
    b) group and interpersonal communication;
    c) setting and achieving goals;
2) to increase self-esteem in young women, allowing them to realize their full potential in Poland's young democratic society;

---

1 For more information on Peace Corps Partnership Program (PCPP) proposals, please refer to the PCPP Volunteers Handbook available from the PCPP coordinator at your post.

3) to explore the idea of democracy and women's abilities to participate in and influence governmental and civil structures;

4) to promote tolerance and the appreciation of diverse peoples especially in light of the global society upon the beginning of the new millennium;

5) to simulate a realistic environment to exemplify ways to ensure equal rights among humans and gender-equal policies within governments and civil society organizations;

to utilize an English speaking atmosphere to improve confidence and encourage language development.

Purpose of project:

Following the enormous success of Camp GLOW – Poland, 1997 and 1998, the purpose of this grant is to support a tradition of excellence by providing the means to implement Camp GLOW 1999 (Ready for the New Millennium!). Poland remains a fledgling democracy despite its 11-year history and the best way to encourage development is to educate Poland's youth about how to influence policy and society. This can best be done by voicing concerns through participation in all aspects of community and governance, through pro-activity, and realizing that one's actions can make a difference. For the most part, women especially, take a passive stance to decisionmaking due to Poland's tradition of Communist style governance and its patriarchal society. Camp GLOW intends to teach young women to be proactive and take an assertive control over their lives and futures through sessions on self-esteem, goal setting, leadership, team-building, healthy living, and self-defense, to name a few.

Justification for the grant:

Poland is a country of rapid change and development and has reaped the benefits of democratic transitions over the past 11 years. However, change does not always come easily and benefits are not always distributed evenly. Despite decreasing levels of unemployment, Polish women, especially, are still suffering from low levels of employment, less opportunity for education, and less chance for employment and/or promotion. Overall, the unemployment rate has dropped from 14.9% in 1995 to 10.3% in 1998. However, the number of unemployed men has dropped significantly (from 1,343,000 to 983,900) and only slightly for women (from 1,495,000 to 1,375,600)[2]. Furthermore, the largest group of unemployed people are between the ages of 15–24, accounting for 29.5% of all unemployed women in 1996. Of all the registered unemployed people in 1996, 58.3% were women. In terms of education, only 32% of Polish women have completed their secondary education and only 7% have university degrees. These statistics are discouraging to the younger generations of women and may lead them to believe that the struggle to become educated and eligible for a professional career is not worth the effort. These young women need to be motivated and introduced to ways to face obstacles that past generations of Polish women did not encounter.

In comparison to the rest of the country, southeastern Poland is not as rapidly transforming because few big cities are in the region and agriculture and small businesses predominate in the economic sphere. For example, 63% of the population in the Zamosc region are employed in the agricultural sector. This portion of the economy is suffering as large multi-national companies are squeezing the profits of local farmers. As the prices for consumer goods continue to rise, the costs of produce and agricultural outputs are decreasing or remain stagnant. Opportunities are limited for women from the rural villages that prevail in this region of Poland due to economic constraints. Camp GLOW will offer economically

---

2 These numbers show the decreasing rate of unemployment among men and women from 1994 to 1996.

challenged, rural youth the opportunity to leave home and attend a summer camp which for some campers may be their first vacation away from home.

The restructuring of Poland's provinces, decreasing the number from 49 to 16, will result in an increased opportunity for governance at a decentralized level, giving way to more positions of local authority for Poland's citizens. This is an opportunity for more women, and men, to participate in democratic governance. Becoming aware of the new system of governance is important to the younger generation so that they will be confident and knowledgeable as they reach the professional world. The qualities of a successful person in this atmosphere include high self-esteem, motivation, pro-activity, flexibility, dedication, and a desire to work hard to succeed. At Camp GLOW, young women will learn about various elements of democracy and have the opportunity to develop the characteristics that will make them successful in the future. Empowerment and encouragement to explore one's personal qualities and assets will be a central theme in the sessions of GLOW 1999. These sessions will be designed to prepare young women for life in the 21st Century so that they can take an active part within a new democratic society and turn dreams into reality.

Camp GLOW 1999 will offer its campers a realistic setting in which to explore the various aspects of democracy in ways that will prove meaningful to the young women at present and in the future. The campers will take part in a simulation of a meeting between "government representatives" of various CEE nations. During the week, the girls will select to represent one of the following nations during a mock UN Regional Conference on Women (to be molded after the actual UN World Conference on Women, Beijing, 1995): Poland, Slovakia, Ukraine, Bulgaria, Romania, Hungary, Czech Republic, Macedonia, or Albania. The campers will prepare a statement on the status of women in their particular countries and then campaign, lobby, and merge their ideas into a regional statement on the status of women in Central and Eastern Europe. The issues to be addressed in the final document will include: gender equal status, women's rights in the workplace, equal pay for equal work, safeguards against sexual harassment and domestic violence, health care specifically for women's needs, and other forms of discrimination. Presenting their final project to an actual panel of women working presently in the field of women in development (representatives from the Women's Association for Gender Equal Status) will add authenticity to their experience with democratic procedures.

Lastly, Camp GLOW will include several types of physical empowerment activities. In a high stress environment, the ability to relax and depend upon inner strength to face obstacles is of utmost importance. For this reason, the campers will be taught relaxation and stress relief techniques, kickboxing for endurance and strength building, and self-defense to increase confidence and self-reliance. These skills are every more important as an influx of western values (as seen in the media and entertainment industries, especially) influence the ideas of youth in terms of body image and social behavior. A healthy mind, body, and attitude coupled with individuality, independence, and self-reliance are attributes significant to today's Polish youth. It is a confusing time as a new generation encounters decisions that have not been faced by their mentors (mothers, grandmothers, teachers, etc). Camp GLOW can help instill confidence, support new ideas, provide resources and awareness to existing opportunities, and motivate to make a difference in the lives of its participants.

Other Remarks

- Recruitment of campers will take place in the spring of 1999. The English departments of several high schools in southeastern Poland will be contacted and asked to nominate two or three young women for consideration as participants in GLOW '99. These young women should demonstrate characteristics of leadership, enthusiasm for learning, and teamwork. They should be in the second or third year of school with a four or five grade average in English class. Intermediate and advanced English skills will be preferred.

- Camp GLOW is a sustainable project in that a "Club GLOW" will be formed to keep the girls united after the camp ends. The Camp GLOW 1998 participants accomplished this and the 1999 campers will have an opportunity to continue this tradition.
  - Four Polish students currently attending NKJO (studying to be English teachers) will serve as junior counselors. Before and during the camp, the junior counselors will be trained in the organization, implementation, and facilitation of Camp GLOW, thus preparing them to replicate the camp in the future.

SAMPLE BUDGET

Percentage of the project's costs which the requested grant would cover: 74%

Project contributions expected from other sources: Paper, water, pens, photocopies, name badges, other office supplies for preparation, medical supplies, books (prizes), T-shirts, staff transportation.

USDC Funding Requested:	Local Currency	US Dollars
Lodging/Food	13,230.00	3,780
7 nights lodging plus 3 meals daily for 40 participants and 14 staff members x local currency		
2 nights before camp for 10 staff (preparation)	700	200
1 night after camp for 10 staff (conclusion)	350	100
Subtotal	**14,280.00**	**4,080**
Transportation		
Participants	2640	754
Counselors/Staff	*1000*	*286*
Guests	450	129
Subtotal	**4,090**	**1,169**
Materials		
Art Supplies	250	71
T-shirts (54 units@ local currency)	*540*	*154*
Postage	250	71
Film/Developing	300	86
Additional		
Snacks	500	143
Prizes	*300*	*86*
First-Aid Kit	*100*	*29*
Subtotal	**2,440**	**697**
Grand Total	**20,810.00**	**5,946**
TOTAL AMOUNT REQUESTED FROM PCPP	**18,870.00**	**5,391**

Italicized line items have been subtracted as they are expected as contributions from other sources.

Congratulations!

On this 28th day of July year 2000, we hereby acknowledge that

_____

has successfully completed Camp GLOW, a weeklong self-empowerment leadership camp for young women conducted in English.

Your hard work reflects that you are a confident, courageous, and compassionate woman. The success of your future depends only upon you, your dreams, and your aspirations.

_____
Director

_____
Group Counselor

Girls Leading Our World
Camp GLOW

Congratulations!

You have successfully completed Camp GLOW, an eight day, self-empowerment camp organized specifically for young women.

Your hard work has proven that you are an independent, strong-willed, and confident woman. The success of your future depends only upon you and your dreams and aspirations.

_____

Participant Name

The counselors of Camp GLOW wish you the strength and encouragement to accomplish your goals!

counselors' signatures

STRENGTH * UNITY * POWER

Girls Leading Our World
Camp GLOW

APPENDIX J

EVALUATION FORM – CAMP GLOW POLAND

1. What was your favorite session/activity during Camp GLOW? Why? Circle your top 3 choices:

ATTITUDES	KAYAKING	JOURNAL WRITING
SELF-ESTEEM, SEXUAL	HARASSMENT	HIKE
SELF-PORTRAITS	CAREER PLANNING	GOAL SETTING
SKITS	VALUES	DIVERSITY
EXPLORING	BODY MAPPING	PANEL
ELECTIONS/CONGRESS	EXPRESSING OURSELVES	LEADERSHIP
BREAST CANCER AWARENESS	HEALTHY LIFESTYLES	

2. If you could change anything about Camp GLOW, what would it be and why?

3. What is the most important/interesting thing you learned? The least interesting?

4. How did you feel about the level of English?

    a. No problem   b. Sometimes difficult   c. Very difficult

5. Do you think this camp should be in Polish? Why or why not?

6. How has Camp GLOW changed or not changed your ideas/feelings about women's lives in Poland? Please describe.

7. Please tell us your honest opinion about Camp GLOW: rate Camp GLOW on a scale of 1–10 with 10 being positive and 1 being negative. Why?

8. What did you think of the campsite for GLOW '99? (Again, rate it on a scale from 1 to 10.) Explain.

9. Would you be willing to pay to attend Camp GLOW, if you had the chance to participate in a future camp?

10. Additional comments or suggestions:

COMPILATION OF CAMP EVALUATIONS
POLAND

1. **What were your favorite sessions during Camp GLOW?**

The top three sessions were:
   1. Stress and Relaxation (27 votes)
   2. Self-esteem (20 votes)
   3. Hiking (16 votes)

Other popular sessions: kick-boxing/self defense, goal setting, tolerance and diversity, team-building and doll-making.

2. **If you could change anything about Camp GLOW, what would it be and why?**

- More free time
- Longer breaks
- More sports, more hiking
- Shorter/fewer sessions
- Sessions outside
- Everything was perfect, wouldn't change a thing

3. **What is the most important/interesting thing you learned? The least important/interesting?**

Most interesting/important thing learned – to be free, to have self-esteem, to be more self-confident, to take care of my health, to be creative, to listen to others, about women's rights, goal setting, diversity, self-defense, relaxation, doll-making, understanding myself and others, speaking English all the time, and making new friends.
"I am a woman and can do everything I want."
"I am a phenomenal woman."
"I am an important person and I should love and respect myself."
"I've learned that all people are special and they possess inner beauty."
"Camp changed my opinion of Americans."

Least interesting/important thing learned – Doll-making, hiking, healthy lifestyles, women's rights conference, and attitudes.

4. **How did you feel about the level of English?**

No problem – 27%
Sometimes difficult – 70%
Very difficult – 2%

5. **Do you think this camp should be in Polish? Why or why not?**

Yes – 43%
No – 54%
Don't know – 2%

6. **How has Camp GLOW changed (or not changed) your ideas and feelings about women's lives in Poland? Please describe….**

    I learned that women can change their situations and have higher self-esteem.

    Before Camp GLOW, I never realized or thought about the problems that women face. Now I know I can help the situation.

    "I believe in myself now and know that women can do many good things for society."

    "When I was little, I wanted to be a boy, because I thought that it's easier in this world to be a man. Now I'm proud to be a woman. I know how I can fight for my rights, I can protect myself, I can be more responsible."

    "Now, I think that we women of Poland are able to change our situation, we don't have to be victims, we can do everything on our own, by ourselves! We are strong."

    "I believe that I'm a phenomenal and important person. I now know my place in life."

7. **Please give us your honest opinion about Camp GLOW: Rate Camp GLOW on a scale of 1 to 10, with 10 being the most positive and 1 being the most negative. Why?**

    | 10 – 32% | 9 – 49% | 8 – 16% | 7 – 2% |

    Everything was great! Only, there wasn't enough free time and sessions sometimes were too long.

8. **What did you think of the campsite for GLOW '99? (Again, rate it on a scale from 1 to 10.) Explain.**

    | 10 – 59% | 9 – 16% | 8 – 22% | 7 – 2% |

    Food was great. I love the mountains. Very beautiful and quiet. Wonderful, kind people. Clean house, near everything.

9. **Would you be willing to pay to attend Camp GLOW, if you had the chance to participate in future camp?**

    | a) yes – 22% | b) no – 2% | c) partially – 54% | d) not sure – 22% |

10. **Additional comments or suggestions:**

    "Everything was planned perfectly. I liked all the counselors. I made some great friends. I've learned a lot."

    "The camp should be longer. I think there should be more people from other countries at camp. I would like to meet their traditions."

    "Everything was very, very, very good."

    "I will remember this camp for many years."

    "There should be a camp like this for boys. They have to learn that women are also human."

    "I am really very happy that I could attend this camp. I think it should be organized in the future."

    "The sessions were wonderful. They weren't boring because they were in English and all the time I had to think about the session and the topic."

    "I didn't know that so many girls can live in the same house in Poland, like an oasis."

APPENDIX M

HOW TO FORM A GLOW CLUB IN YOUR SCHOOL

1. **Why have Club GLOW in our schools?**

    - Good for every young woman to gain knowledge
    - Good for society
    - Helps young women meet people from other schools
    - Helps young women know themselves and improve self-esteem
    - Improve English
    - Teach young women to be strong

2. **Meetings in Big School/Clubs in Small Schools**

    - For secondary school students aged 15–19 or no division by age, one club in the school
    - Males and females invited to participate
    - English and LANGUAGE can be used at meetings
    - Each club decides how often they will meet
    - One or two camps a year (one in summer, one during school year)

3. **Meeting Ideas**

    - Talk about goals, careers, values (what's important to us)
    - Tell others what we have learned at Camp GLOW
    - Sports, games, music, party, HAVE FUN!
    - Meet with other groups, clubs
    - Read books, magazines and discuss
    - Talk about everyday problems and new experiences
    - Watch movies (for example, *Fried Green Tomatoes, Thelma & Louise*)
    - Practice English
    - Talk about self-esteem
    - Guest speakers/mentors
    - Translate poetry, songs
    - Sleepover/Slumber party

4. **How to Keep in Touch**

    - Letters among clubs
    - Phone calls
    - Birthday/Name day postcards
    - E- mail to each other
    - Create a web page
    - Meetings

5. **Main Club Responsibilities**

    - Newsletter
    - Organize mid-year Camp GLOW
    - Work with a Peace Corps Volunteer
    - Fund-raising activities (discos, making postcards, make/sell sandwiches, bake sales, concerts, car washes, sell Camp GLOW magazine)

6. **Goals**

    - Find interested people
    - Share what we did at Camp GLOW and spread information
    - Have meetings, establish deadlines (have food & drink at meetings!)
    - Teach self-esteem

SAMPLE THANK YOU NOTES
FROM VOLUNTEERS AND CAMPERS

Dear Friend of Camp GLOW,

While July 7–14 might seem like a long time ago, for those of us who participated in Camp Girls Leading Our World the memory is still very fresh.

We have been meaning to get our thank-you notes out but we had to wait until all the counselors could meet to hold our camp evaluation session, which we did recently.

Thank you so much for your contribution to one of the most wonderful experiences we have ever had. The superlatives could go on and on for the amazing event that Camp GLOW was for both campers and counselors alike. It was a magical time of sharing, growth and fun. Over the course of one week friendships were made, horizons broadened, and new leaders were created!

We are including a camp photo, a summary of some of our activities and a thank-you letter written by one of the participants. There doesn't seem to be a way to capture all the emotions that come out of GLOW but we want you to know that your contribution changed lives! Our campers will never forget GLOW and for us it was the highlight of our Peace Corps service.

Thank you so much!

NAME

——

Dear GLOW Friend,

I want to thank you for everything you have done for me, for your great support and contribution.

Camp GLOW was a great and wonderful experience for me. Here I learned a lot of useful things that will help me in the future like trust, trust people, help each other, to communicate, to be honest and to work in a team. Here I learned what means friendship in our life, what it means to set a goal and to achieve it. During this week I became more stronger, I learned and discovered a lot of things about myself. Now I have more confidence in myself and I can do whatever I want.

I found out and I understood that a woman can be a great leader for her community and having a strong character she can improve her community and make it a better place to live.

I know you did a lot of sacrifices to make this camp become a reality and I want to thank you for this.

Thank you for the great time I've spent here and for the interesting things I learned.

With respect,

NAME
GLOW camper